# Socially Wize Parenting

## The No-Fuss Simple Approach to Parenting

By Tracey D. Pugh, M.ED

Copyright © 2019 by Tracy Pugh

All rights reserved. In accordance with the U.S. Copyright Act of 1976, the scanning, uploading and electronic sharing of any part of the book without the permission of the author or publisher constitutes unlawful piracy and theft of the author's intellectual property. If you would like to use material from the book (other than for review purposes), prior written permission must be obtained by contacting author @ tracey@sociallywize.com

Walton Publishing House, Houston, Texas

Printed in the United States of America

Disclaimer: The advice and strategies found within may not be suitable for every situation. This work is sold with the understanding that neither the author nor the publisher are held responsible for the results accrued from the advice in this book.

Library of Congress Cataloging-in-Publication Data has been applied for.

ISBN : 978-1-7330208-0-0

# Dedication

I would like to thank the many people who have made this book possible:

First, to my husband and my children – Trey, it has been the biggest blessing of my life to raise our children together with you. Jacob and Jessica, you are my daily inspirations and my reason for wanting to be a better person every single day. I love you.

To my parents – you are truly the "wind beneath my wings." You have consistently shown me what unconditional love is and what being a dedicated parent looks like. You were my first teachers and I appreciate your unselfish love and commitment in raising Sade' and I.

To my sister circle – My baby sister Sade', my first-cousins who have always been my rocks, Dawn, Delight, Karen, Monica, Janice, Sonja and Tymesia – thank you for believing in me and pushing me to do my very best at all times.

To Telea and the Phenixx Marketing Group – thank you for believing in my vision and helping me realize my potential. Love you my forever friend!

To Dr. Sherrie Walton- Walton Publishing House – thank you for the many hours of "blood, sweat and tears" along with me. Thank you for your patience, support and guidance. None of this would be possible without you!

# Chapters

| | | |
|---|---|---|
| Chapter 1: | Socially Wize Parenting | 1 |
| Chapter 2: | The Role of Parents | 10 |
| Chapter 3: | Setting Realistic Expectations | 21 |
| Chapter 4: | Parenting Different Personalities | 30 |
| Chapter 5: | Healthy Boundaries | 48 |
| Chapter 6: | Communicating with Your child | 53 |
| Chapter 7: | Understanding Your Child's Cues | 60 |
| Chapter 8: | The ABC's of Discipline | 72 |
| Chapter 9: | Raising a Responsible Child | 82 |
| Chapter 10: | Resolving Conflict | 92 |
| Chapter 11: | Health & Wellness | 101 |
| Chapter 12: | The Tough Issues | 108 |
| Chapter 13: | Affirm your child | 119 |
| Index 1: | A-Z Cheat Sheet | 129 |
| Index 2: | Family Fun For All Ages | 135 |
| Index 3: | Socially Wize Parent Assessment | 160 |

About the Author

## SociallyWize Parenting Pledge

I will do my best to:
- Love my child unconditionally.
- Treat my child with patience, respect, and kindness.
- Provide support as my child receives the best education that I can provide.
- Allow my child to explore his/her own interests.
- Recognize that making mistakes is an important part of learning.
- Travel together and introduce my child to as many cultures as possible.
- Sit down for a meal together as a family at least once a day.
- Laugh a lot.
- Find pleasure in the small things as well as big life events.
- Surround ourselves with a supportive community of family and friends.
- Live an active and healthy lifestyle.

# Chapter 1

# Socially Wize Parenting

*"Children have never been very good at listening to their elders, but they have never failed to imitate them." - James Baldwin*

I can remember the lines that formed on my elementary school playground as students stood patiently waiting for their turn to ask me how to solve their problems. I collected their 25 cents and in return I helped *fix their life*. It was at that early age I realized I had a gift for listening and solving problems. At eight years old I had discovered my purpose, and for me, it was about more than just giving counsel (as best as an eight-year-old could). It was about seeing my classmates happy. Back then I learned people needed solutions and there was always a way to solve the problem. Fast forward to today, I have honed those skills and I am proud to have helped hundreds of families find solutions to some of their toughest problems. This book will share my experiences with both children and adults and proven techniques to help you become effective with raising your child. It will also highlight some of the effective methods I have introduced to other families just like yours.

I consider myself a hands-on expert in parenting and children for a few reasons. First, I have been involved in education for over 18 years, both as a consultant and as a teacher. I am in the classroom every day observing children's behavior, offering support, counsel and education. *Yes, it is true children emulate what they see at home.* Second, my husband and I have raised two successful children who are currently enrolled in college applying what we have taught them in the home. I was blessed with a son and a daughter with two different personality types (we'll talk more about that later) and I am a survivor! Lastly, I am an avid lifelong learner, always studying the dynamics of both children and parents. I enjoy implementing new techniques to foster better results.

Today's families come together in many ways: natural birth, marriage, adoption, surrogacy, and everything in between. No matter how your family was formed, as parents we have been blessed with the amazing and scary responsibility of raising a child. If you have been a parent for longer than a day, you may have discovered that parenting isn't a bed of roses or a walk in the park on a sunny day. If you hear other parents saying they have it all figured out, *run* far away from them. Yes, parenting can be an amazing experience filled with great memories and milestones, but it is hard work when done properly. Many parents aren't trained in what to do or how to do it and usually end up frustrated with the process. Parenting is learned on the job. This is why I wrote *Socially Wize Parenting*. My passion is to help parents overcome the fears and disappointments that can be experienced in parenting. I still hold on to the traditional value that families are our bedrock. Tight-knit families produce strong legacies and in return create socially and consciously aware children prepared to enter the world. With the proper 'applied' knowledge, parenting can be a rewarding experience for both parents and children. While no two families are alike, some principles in parenting are universal. It is one of the most profound and meaningful endeavors of our lives. In parenting we are pushed out of our comfort zone day after day, tested and made uncomfortable in ways we never imagined, but most of us would do it all over again in a heartbeat. Our children are worth every drop of our blood, sweat, and tears.

In my many conversations with parents, two main themes emerge. First, parents acknowledge they want to create a harmonious home that is peaceful. They want their homes to be nurturing and warm environments that bring out the best in each family member. Second, parents express the desire for their children to grow into mature individuals. They want their children to establish a sense of commitment to their own lives, to the people around them, and to help them develop the skills necessary to act in responsible and respectful ways. My hope is through the development of healthy self-disciplined children, families will become empowered to enjoy happy, meaningful, and authentic lives. Now let's pause here. I don't want to mislead you into believing implementing these values will be as simple as they read on these pages. It will require work from all members of the family. It will also require that we as parents step up to the plate and be willing to expand our knowledge about what it takes to make our family dynamic work. In addition, creating a harmonious home and supporting confident children requires that we as parents first become more confident ourselves. With intentional practice, our own self-awareness, self-regulation, and self-confidence will co-evolve and support these qualities in our children. By seeing confidence as a loving vessel for ideal development, we can grow and learn together. We learn the value of respect and cooperation by experiencing teamwork in the home. This is where we experience firsthand both how personal responsibility is empowering and how it helps to create a safe and restful place where all family members can thrive. It is the relationship—the framework of love and respect—that motivates us beyond our personal needs and desires and inspires the development of confidence.

I must warn you, while there are some things that can

be absorbed through text, when it comes to the parent-child interaction, there are no textbooks, no written tests, no diplomas and degrees that can form a healthy relationship. This bond only comes through experience and sorting through life's many demands. When you put in work you finally reap the satisfaction of strong and loving bonds. Socially Wize Parenting echoes many of the apprehensions of everyday parenting. This book offers suggestions, solutions, and most importantly, food for thought for all those for whom being a parent, or a guardian is a demanding, dynamic and immensely rewarding role. This resource is for all parents, guardians and caregivers and those that support them.

At Socially Wize, our method is an intentional yet flexible approach to raising children. I have found it most effective to focus on principles, rather than trying to apply techniques not rooted in deeper understanding when young emotional minds are involved. It's no secret that there are so many emotions that children experience, and it would not be wise to solely rely on their reactions to gauge the effectiveness of our parenting. "Emotional competence undergoes dramatic changes within the first five years of life." Journal of Applied Developmental Psychology, Volume 45, July–August 2016. The guiding premise is that our role as parents is to discern what sustenance (emotional, physical, spiritual) is needed, moment by moment, and to provide the nourishment that nature needs to help our children bloom into their full potential. This book will support you in becoming the most trustworthy, flexible, and intuitive gardener-parent you can be.

We have also found that what is most important is not to try to be perfect, but rather to allow space for the messes and imperfections, and to practice holding them in a context of self-confidence. When our children were in Pre-K and first grade, I remember trying to be the perfect "Super Mom!" I wanted to make sure that our children never wanted for anything and never felt left out or sad if there was an opportunity for their parent to be volunteers in the classroom or on a field trip, despite the fact that both my husband and I were working full-time. I had the dreaded "Mommy Guilt." Lucky for me, right before the Thanksgiving holiday, my daughter's Pre-K teacher asked me if I could volunteer to discuss and share Kwanzaa with the class before school let out for the upcoming winter holiday break. I was thrilled, over the moon, doing the 'moonwalk' with excitement! Finally, it was my turn to volunteer in class and be "That Mom!" Unfortunately there was a slight problem. While although we are African-American, our family does not celebrate Kwanzaa. We celebrate Christmas proudly and have nothing but the utmost respect for Kwanzaa. Despite these facts, I was still too elated to finally have the opportunity to share with the class.

I ran immediately to the public library, checked out every book on Kwanzaa, raced home to tell my husband, called my mother and shared the great news with my closest girlfriends. I was finally on the map! I was going to be like all of the other moms. After I had fed the family dinner, helped with bath time and bedtime routines, I tucked in our daughter and said good-night. I hugged her tightly and then said with excitement, "Jessica! Guess what? Mommy is going to come into YOUR class and talk about Kwanzaa with you and all of your friends!" I was beaming from ear to ear. Jessica, with her child-like grace, looked at me with joy and big doe eyes and said, "Oh yeah! That's great, Mommy! I can't wait. But wait, who is Kwanzaa? Our cousin?" I didn't know how to respond. My joyful, excited bubble had just been burst by my four-year-old precious daughter. How in the world could I stand in front of a group of children and pretend to share something that I knew absolutely nothing about? Sure, I could use this as an opportunity to teach the children and myself something new – but would it be meaningful? Would the time that I so desperately wanted to share with the class be a true definition of myself and my family? No. I had gotten so caught up with wanting to be "one of the cool moms who volunteered often" that I almost missed an opportunity to use my time to be meaningful, intentional and authentic.

I hugged Jessica tight, and we discussed sharing our family's Christmas traditions (some of the yummy food, special stories, and family habits that we felt were special) – instead of discussing a holiday that no one in our family knew a lot about. The next day, I had to swallow my pride, approach the Pre-K teacher and let her know that I had responded in haste. That we did not celebrate Kwanzaa, but that Jessica and I had discussed some things that we would be willing to share with the class. The teacher apologized for making the assumption that because we were African-American, that we would know a lot about the holiday. She agreed that our special family traditions on the holiday that we did celebrate would be more meaningful to discuss. Over the next few weeks, Jessica and I spent time together planning out what we wanted to share. It ended up being a phenomenal time for me and for the class.

That was a valuable lesson learned and one I considered a milestone in my parenting. Becoming aware of our parenting patterns and reactions can be quite painful, and it is essential to bring an open, nonjudgmental heart to as many moments as we can. When we hold our difficult feelings—even the seemingly unforgivable ones— with compassion, we set the stage for healing and growth. As parents, we must learn to trust ourselves. I want you to sit back and relax as you read this book. This should feel like a safe place for you to learn and explore. I want you to consider me a trusted friend and advisor. There should be no judgement or guilt as you read through these chapters. My intent is not for you to feel as if you are a bad parent or like you've been failing at this. Yes, we as parents are far from perfect, but our love and commitment are cavernous. Trust yourself. Trust your child and his/her process.

Socially Wize Parenting holds many universal truths that are contained within us all but are often forgotten in the hurly-burly of everyday parenting. Devoid of judgements, this book was written to help you draw upon your innate wisdom. This book is offered as a reminder that the sustenance your child needs is already in your naturally wise and loving heart. Life has decided that you are exactly who your child needs to reach his/her full potential.

### *How This Book Is Organized*

I will admit, it can be a challenge to write a book for parents. I offer this book with humility and with the knowledge that chaos and challenge will be part of the process. Sometimes you will have the patience of a saint. Other times, you will be pushed over the edge. Please hold our suggestions as a set of best practices, knowing that my team and I are right there with you, stumbling along and making plenty of messes ourselves.

The guidance and associated lingo can get annoying sometimes, but you must understand the foundation. We are changing the way we think, so we must wrap our brains around why. Why do kids have smart mouth comebacks? Why do we get so worked up? Why is it important to change? This book touches on age groups from toddler to teenager. As an educator, who is also a writer and editor, I wrote each chapter to provide key insights on a wide range of topics. There's literally something for every letter of the alphabet: from A for Apologies to Z for Zombies. Since you are now a part of my extended family, I have to tell you that everyone that knows me knows my favorite saying: *"Oh my lanta"* It's my way of expressing surprise or astonishment. You will see this saying throughout the book. This will be a little sign that we're connecting. Let's keep reading and enjoy the journey!

# Chapter 2

# The Role of Parents

*"We never know the love of a parent until we become parents ourselves." - Henry Ward Beecher*

Can you remember how you behaved when you were a child? I can almost guarantee a flood of emotions rush through your body when you reflect on your childhood memories. I often like to have parents reflect on some of the wild and bizarre things they did, to help them not only relate to their child but to understand the role they play in teaching their children how to become responsible citizens. I have so many amusing stories that I could share about my childhood including the time I cut my hair for Show and Tell and tried to glue it back on before the end of the day...*oh my lanta!* We all have our share of embarrassing stories and life lessons.

Now that we are adults we recognize those were phases we went through at the time, that shaped how we saw things through our own innocent eyes. Depending on how we were raised and what we experienced, it may be a bit difficult to step into the role of a parent and understand the part we have in the process. Now let's take this a bit further. What type of home were you raised in? Did you have a healthy relationship with your parents? I grew up in a family where children were seen and not heard. My parents learned from their parents, who learned from theirs and so on. However, with each generation each set of parents had to learn to adapt to where their children could best relate. We can be stubborn and say, "well that's the way I was raised, so that's the way it is." Or we can adapt without compromise of our morals. We shouldn't try to raise our children with outdated rules that no longer apply to where they are today. For example, when I grew up- children spent time outdoors until the street lights came on. We were gone for hours at a time with no adult supervision. When I had children, it was insane for us to let our children out of our line of sight. Someone could have snatched them, or they could have badly hurt themselves. From the time I was a kid to the time my children were kids' society had changed. Those changes reflected how we monitored our children.

As parents we want to see our children thrive: to see them grow into healthy, joyful, emotionally intelligent beings. Our aspiration is to support our children as they grow, learn and evolve. Pause for a moment and feel the wholesomeness and natural goodness of this intention. You care. You love your child. You can trust this. And yet, lived experience is often far removed from this natural and deeply wholesome love. Socially Wize Parenting is an approach to parenting that helps guide us effectively back toward this innate path of love and wisdom. You can't erase what you learned, however, you can intentionally become the person your child will always look to for guidance.

As a responsible parent, you will provide the guidance that helps your children change, grow, and mature. Responsible behavior, in line with your children's maturity levels, is taught and expected. One of the most important parts as a parent is to provide "structure" for your children. In the parent role, you give direction, impose rules, use discipline, set limits, establish and follow through with consequences, hold your children accountable for their behavior, and teach values. There are several benefits to providing structure. For example, when providing structure, your children will feel a sense of security knowing that rules will be in place when they can't control their own impulses – you will be there to stop them, guide them, and be in charge of their well-being.

Having structure also teaches children to endure a reasonable amount of frustration and disappointment when they don't always get their own way. They'll discover that the world does not revolve totally around them and as a result, they become less egocentric. With the proper structure your child will learn responsible behavior, believe that they can actually accomplish goals, learn from their mistakes and gain experience making decisions, become more self-sufficient and capable as they learn the skills to become independent.

Often parents want to be friends with their children instead of wanting to carry out this "structured parent role" in a healthy way. It is vital to your children's development that you discipline them, teach them, guide them, provide rules and follow through on the rules, and set reasonable expectations for their behavior. You do not have to be mean or constantly yell as you set limits. For example, if you sit down with your child to set a schedule for extra-curricular activities, you are providing guidance. If you have your son read three pages of a book aloud to practice his reading skills which his teacher has said are below grade level, you would be providing structure. You may still be a warm and loving interaction, but your goal is to help your child grow and acquire new skills; therefore, you are providing structure. By holding children to standards and helping them to achieve success, you help them to feel capable and thereby build their self-esteem.

### *Be Supportive*

In addition to providing structure, our role as parents is to support nature in growing our children up by providing certain forms of sustenance. The nourishment that children need to become confident falls into five categories of experience: **Unconditional Love, Space, Guidance, Healthy Boundaries, and Mistakes**.

1) **Unconditional love:** Children need to know that they are perfect exactly as they are. When your children know they are loved unconditionally they will build a level of trust and respect that will not be affected even if they don't always make the best choices.

2) **Space:** Your child's personality traits will evolve in stages. As they become more aware of themselves, don't overcrowd them or attempt to mold them into someone else. Give them the space to develop and be themselves as they retain a basic trust in the world and a sense of their inherent value as human beings.

3) **Guidance:** Proper guidance helps children develop impulse control, emotional intelligence, and the ability to acclimate in the face of adversity. There is a difference between guidance and forced control. Guidance is instructional advice that will lead your child to make reasonable and intelligent decisions when they are not in your presence. Attempting to control your child will only be effective when you are in your child's presence.

4) **Healthy boundaries:** Boundaries can easily be crossed when they have not been properly established. Be

careful in leaving this gray area with your child. When they feel a degree of autonomy, children remain curious, engaged, and develop an increasing sense of responsibility over their lives. However, children also need mentorship and healthy boundaries. These two elements communicate to children, "While it is true that you are perfect as you are, it is also true that you have a long way to go." Children have a lot to learn about the world, and it requires a great deal of time, guidance, and practice to develop the skills that comprise healthy self-confidence. Teach your child healthy boundaries for school and play. Also teach them how to give you the necessary boundaries you need as a parent.

**5) Mistakes:** Our mistakes can end up nourishing our children. We write "missed takes" instead of "mistakes" to signify that these are "missed takes"— moments or occasions when we missed the mark and need to correct course. In this way, mistakes can be beneficial and nourishing, rather than simply bad or wrong.

### Provide Security

It's also our role as parents to help our children feel safe and secure. One of the most important qualities you want to instill in your children is a deep sense of security in themselves and in the world. There are three messages you want your children to get to nurture their developing sense of security.

**Others:** There are people in my world who will help me and protect me when needed.

**Self:** I am the boss of all that is me (body, mind, soul) and I am strong enough to handle myself in situations.

**World:** The world/environment that I live in is a safe place that I can explore with confidence and where I can be free from fear of the unknown.

The first message of security involves your children feeling securely attached to YOU – the parent. The operative word with attachment is trust. Simply put, secure attachment develops in children who learn that they can rely on their parents to meet their physical and emotional needs. When they are cold, hungry, or thirsty, they know you are there to provide them with warmth and sustenance. When they are scared, sad, or lonely, they can turn to you for comfort. This attachment isn't just important for you and your children to develop healthy relationships. The perceptions children develop about their relationship with you, the emotions they feel towards and from you, and the experiences your children have with you become the template for relationships they will develop in the future.

Imagine children who grow up without that attachment, trust, and sense of security. They learn that others can't be trusted to care for them. Such a worldview would have a profoundly negative impact on every aspect of their lives, including how they come to see themselves and their emotional life, relationships, and strivings. Who they would ultimately become and what they would eventually do would emerge from this dark place of doubt, fear, and need. Children with insecure attachment experience significant separation anxiety when parents leave, yet find little comfort when the parent returns. They are often described as needy and clingy by teachers and other caregivers. In adulthood, they fear intimacy, have difficulty expressing their emotions, lack trust in their intimate relationships, and take rejection badly.

Now consider children who are raised with a strong feeling of attachment to their parents. They come to view their parents as safe, friendly, and predictable people who they can count on to meet their needs. The view of relationships that they would subsequently develop would be one of comfort, interest, and opportunity. Securely attached children separate from their parents with ease and welcome them back with enthusiasm and are readily calmed by parents when frightened. In adulthood, these children have generally high self-esteem, are socially competent, and are able to establish and maintain intimate relationships, and are emotionally expressive.

Solid family relationships are muddled affairs, and children learn from seeing their parents' authentic struggles with confidence and grit. The times we lose our cool or act unskillfully can create an opening where unpretentiousness, forgiveness, and empathy can bring us closer with our child and grow each of us up in the process. The shadow characteristics of ourselves often lead to the deepest of healing and intimacy. When we recognize our misstep and move to reconnect and repair, both we and our children learn and grow. Your children will appreciate you more when they connect to the example offered to them. Remember your children are impressionable; instead of striving to be perfect, strive to be impactful. Face it — you are an imperfect parent. ***Oh my lanta, we all are!*** You have strengths and weaknesses as a family leader but don't let those weaknesses minimize the role you play in your child's life.

### Encouragement

A parent is their child's first teacher and should remain their best teacher throughout life. You want to encourage your children to explore new things, be free to express their feelings, and feel confident in being themselves. Our kids do not need to be a younger version of ourselves to be successful people. It does not make you a bad parent if your child is not exactly like you! Socially Wize Parents guide their children into being who they were meant to be.

On a scale of 1-10: How effective are you in these areas? 10 being the highest.

Structure and Stability?

Being Supportive?

Providing Security?

Being Encouraging?

Overall, do you provide a safe, supportive and encouraging environment for your child?

If yes, in what ways can you improve?

If no, what are you willing to change today?

Have you been guilty of trying to be the perfect parent? After reading this section, what is the best impact you feel you can have on your child?

# Chapter 3
# Setting Realistic Expectations
(Identifying your Parenting Type)

Do you dream of raising the next Albert Einstein or Barack Obama? Do you have hopes and dreams of your child being drafted by the NFL? It's perfectly alright to have these desires, but is that aspiration what's best for your child? This discussion is not to discourage you from having high expectations for your children. We all want our children to achieve more and do more than we did. But what if you aren't raising a child with an IQ of 170? What do you do? You set realistic expectations, that's what. You take the time to understand the child you are raising and you celebrate them for their strengths instead of criticizing their weaknesses. As parents we must be careful about pushing unrealistic expectations on our children and pressuring them to live up to expectations that we didn't live up to. As an educator I have met many children that are pressured to be so great and they live their lives in constant anxiety and fear. "What will my parents think of me if I bring home a less-than-perfect grade?...What will my father do if I don't make the team?" Children should not feel pressured to be overly high achievers in such a way that it affects them emotionally and mentally. Think about this: How well would you do at your workplace if someone constantly stood over your shoulders pointing out your mistakes? Would it make you uneasy? Children are no different. The more unmerited pressure placed on them, the least likely they will be able to perform. Learn the art of guiding without playing the enforcer role.

As I stated when we first began our journey together, this is a safe and non-judgmental zone. The suggestions I make may seem a bit tough at first, but when you revisit them you will understand the reasoning behind the ideas.. I want to encourage you to have realistic expectations for yourself, your spouse, and your kids. You don't have to have all the answers. In your process learn to be forgiving of yourself if you make a mistake and learn how to forgive your children when they don't measure up to your expectations.

### Identifying your Parenting Type

Research has shown there are five types of parenting:

Instinctive parenting, Attachment, Helicopter, Authoritative, and Permissive parenting. Can you identify below which type best describes you?

***Instinctive Parenting:***

Instinctive Parenting is when parents use their gut or their "instinct" to parent their child. The instinctive parent uses their own personal style of parenting, which has usually been influenced by their upbringing and socialization. An instinctive parent is more likely to teach their child what they know and they parent the way they were parented, regardless of whether they were raised by their mother and father, a single parent, their siblings or another guardian.

**Pros** – Instinctive parents tend to raise their children in an extended-family-like atmosphere, where children have ample opportunity to form close, nurturing relationships with members of all ages. Although most adults do not intend to parent like their own parent, once they become an adult with children, they grow to understand the logic in their parents' methods.

**Cons** – This type of parenting is a repeat of patterns from a previous generational loop. Although repeating patterns are not necessarily a bad thing, there are patterns that can damage another human, especially a small fragile human without developed social skills. Repeating these patterns would be considered detrimental and would need to be addressed professionally.

### *Attachment Parenting:*

Attachment Parenting is a style of parenting that brings out the best in both the child and the parents. Successful Attachment parenting can develop the healthy bond between a parent and a child by helping the baby develop a high level of security and provide a foundation for a healthy parent-child relationship. Attachment parenting allows for mutual sensitivity between the parent and the child. The connected parent can read the body language of the child and redirect the same for a more appropriate behavior. In turn, the child can comprehend the desires and wishes of the parent and act accordingly.

**Pros** – Attachment parenting can develop the mutual shaping of behavior and personality and sensitivity in children. Mutual shaping is demonstrated when you and your child learn to talk to each other. Your behavior, talk, and even thinking will change to your child's level. As you master your child's language, your child will learn to speak the language of the family. Then it will be the child's turn to act, talk, and think at the parents' level.

**Cons** –Attachment parenting could be harmful in the long run. If parents do not punish the child for the sake of attachment, chances of children taking advantage of the situation and doing things on his/her own would be high.

*Helicopter Parenting:*

Out of love and affection for our children, we tend to hover, controlling every small action. While it is imperative to take care of the safety of your child, it is equally important to understand that children learn best in unconstrained natural environments. Children must be given the freedom to discover and make choices. *It is not a good idea to form a transparent safeguard around your child and filter bad people/ situations out of his life.* We should not just give good things as choices to our children. Selecting good things out of bad will help improve their flexibility. Ultimately, they must face the world and real-life conditions, which might be either good or bad.

**Pros** – In order to prevent anything bad from happening, helicopter parents spend almost all their time with their child. They spend so much time together that it allows the parent and child to bond and form a close relationship. By having such a close relationship, the parents can then be involved in every aspect of their child's life, therefore always knowing that he is safe.

**Cons** – This type of parenting is an extreme form of overprotectiveness. Helicopter parenting is often fear-based, and does not allow children to think or act for themselves, resulting in the child losing their sense of independence. In my opinion, helicopter parenting can result in the child rebelling down the road.

### *Authoritative Parenting:*

Authoritarians are the strictest parenting model. Expectations are high, while rewards and displays of affection are minimal. And whereas so many modern parents are concerned with offering choices in lieu of punishment, authoritarian parents have no such compulsions. There is simply no tolerance for misbehavior. For authoritarian parents, there is little in the way of explaining why rules need to be followed, except that they must be followed.

**Pros** -- Children can know what is expected of them and also know why those expectations are in place. In this style of parenting they feel free to ask questions and voice opinions, even if they do not agree with the thoughts of the parents. Notedly, children incrementally take on responsibilities that are age appropriate and are within the scope of their abilities. They choose to obey parents more out of respect and less out of fear of punishment.

**Cons** -- In this style of parenting there is an additional responsibility on the parents. Since the house rules are somewhat broad and don't cover every conceivable situation, parents sometimes find themselves having to develop a completely new response to something the child says or does. This can be difficult to maintain when faced with a particularly willful child. You should know a high degree of patience must be cultivated if the parents are to maintain an authoritative atmosphere in the home. Authoritative parenting requires periodic review and refinement to continue benefiting the children as they grow and their needs change. House rules relevant at age six may be hindrances by age eight. Parents must be alert to the need to modify and amend the rules when necessary, rather than clinging to the same rules year after year.

### *Permissive:*

Permissive parents rarely discipline their children. They avoid confrontation whenever possible. Instead of setting rules and expectations or trying to prevent problems, they choose to instead let children figure things out for themselves.

**Pros** – Communication can be more of a two-way street since parents and child both have a say and children do not feel nervous speaking their minds. Because children know their parents will love them unconditionally—whether they mess up or not—their self-esteem may be higher than other children's. Children are often encouraged to be creative, which can lead to the development of more hobbies and can spark imagination. Conflict is minimized since parents tend to work around their child and their wants and needs.

**Cons** – Some studies have found that this type of parenting style can lead to risky behavior in older children, especially pertaining to alcohol use. "A permissive parenting style and beer drinking are risk factors for alcohol abuse among late adolescents and young adults," one study says. It can also cause kids to internalize their feelings rather than letting them out. One study found that it can affect children as young as age four.

Children develop no sense of boundaries since their parents react to their actions rather than impose sanctions in advance. Children don't always understand the concept of respect since they tend not to defer to their parents or treat them with more reverence. This can especially become difficult in school, work, and other social settings. They're not used to hearing "no," so they can sometimes lash out when they hear so from authority or adults outside of their home.

## Is there a such thing as bad parenting?

We have all heard that bad kids come from bad parents, and I do believe that there are several ways to be a bad parent. Since parents are a child's first teachers in life, a child's attitude, views, goals, and perspective depend on what he or she learns from their parents. A child's demeanor is also a reflection of how they've been treated by their parents. What a child learns or experiences in their early years is known to leave a lasting impression on them. Therefore good parenting is an absolute necessity.

Whenever a child makes a mistake or displays bad manners, the blame is mostly put on the parents because they are responsible for teaching their children how to behave. When a child's bad behavior or emotional state are linked to his or her parents' actions, it is natural to wonder if the parents made a mistake or if they are simply bad parents.

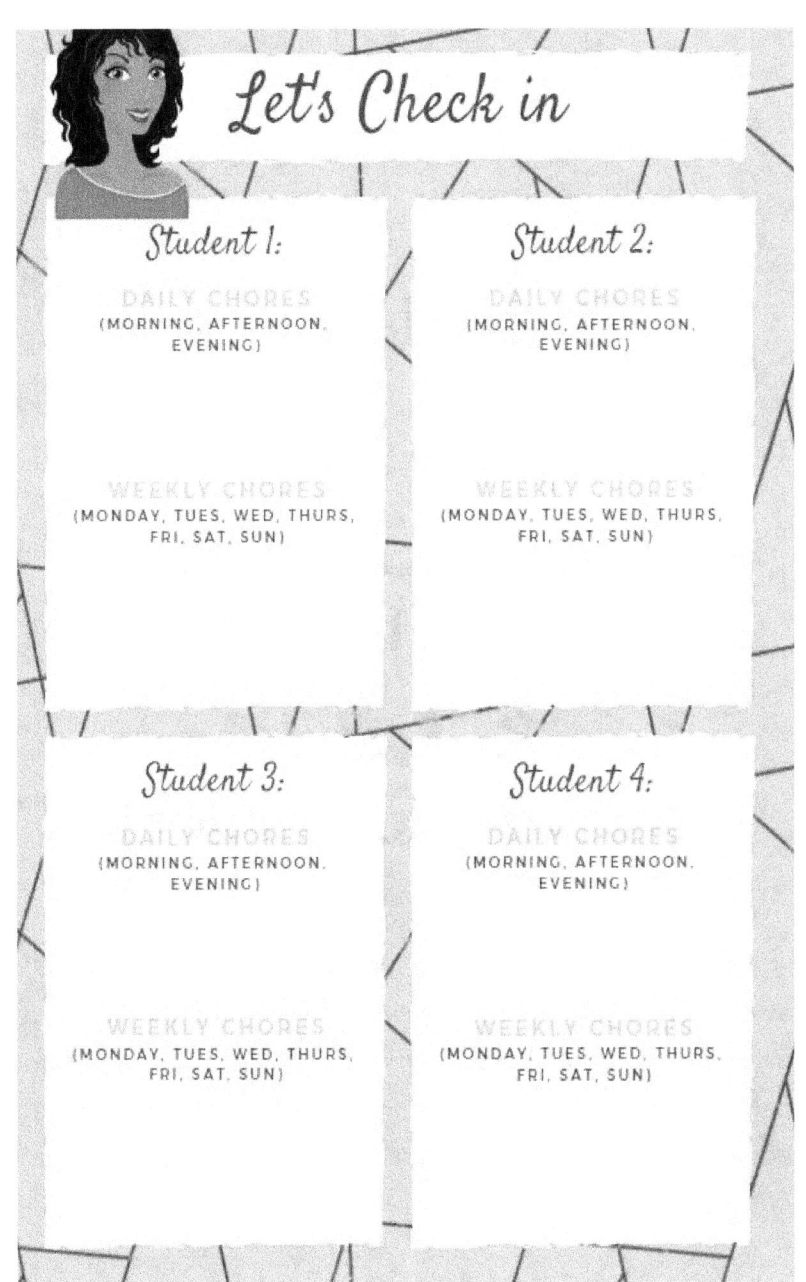

The No-Fuss Simple Approach to Parenting

# Chapter  4

# Your Child's Personality Type & Traits
## (Child vs. Parent)

In my opinion, families are a lot like fudge. Mostly sweet with a few nuts. Most parents are doing the best they can with what they have. They are trying to raise kids from babies in diapers all the way through those funny childhood, adolescence, and teenage years. It is hard. It is at times insane but it can be done.

Being a parent and bringing up children is not an easy

job, in fact in many ways it is the hardest job you may ever have because there is such a wealth of contradictory advice and information available. You may discover that friends and family all want to share with you the benefit of their advice, gleaned from many years of experience of bringing up children, but ultimately the way you raise your children and help your family to grow and develop is up to you (and your partner), your own morals, standards, boundaries, ideas and plans for the future of you and your children.

It is often tough to know exactly what parenting methods and styles to adopt and you may find that you are questioning yourself on a regular basis about certain aspects of your child's development. This is never helped by spending too much time with competitive friends who may appear to be well meaning with their tips and advice, but who can also make life even more stressful. There is no doubt that the way we bring up our children is definitely changing, and while your parents and grandparents may have had one style of parenting, this may not fit in well with the expectations you now have as a parent yourself.

In our last chapter we learned about your parenting style. Now let's identify the type of child you're parenting.

**Energetic: the wild child, always moving child**
**vs.**
**The laid-back parent who just wants to drink coffee without being disturbed**

**What you need to know**

This is your child's disposition; he/she doesn't bounce around and beg for attention just to bother you. "Personality is inborn, but how you guide and respond to children can influence their personalities and how well they get along in the world," says Tanya Altmann, MD, a clinical professor of pediatrics at UCLA and author of the American Academy of Pediatrics' *Mommy Calls*.

**What you can do**

First of all, try not to suppress your child's robust feelings, even if they get on your nerves. Telling your child to "calm down" could make them feel insecure and excluded. Instead, take a deep breath and try to phrase your comments along the lines of, "Aw, sweetheart, I see how disappointed you are; it is obvious that this situation is really upsetting you." Then give them a schedule and set limits. Laid-back parents often do not provide enough structure for a child who is Type A. Your child should already know the rules you have established for everyone that lives in your home; your child should have a routine and idea of when to expect mealtime and bedtime. Most children are more comfortable and feel like they have a sense of control when they know what's expected and what comes next. Even within the structure of the established rules, your child will still have the freedom to become be who he/she will be. Your job as a parent is to think beyond your own personality to accommodate your child when possible. Just as you schedule time for school and extracurricular activities, make sure that you schedule time for your child to have free play that can mix active and, ideally, outdoor play to blow off any pent-up frustrations and energy. You may have to speed up your laid-back tempo when you are with your child during these times. Also, try relaxing activities that you can do with your child. Yoga, tai-chi, taekwondo, painting, and meditation classes are a few ideas that can possibly calm both child and parent and keep everyone in control.

**Disorderly: The unorganized, can't find anything child**

**vs.**

**The obsessively color-coded whiteboard schedule parent**

**What you need to know**

Many children go through a disorderly phase, but it doesn't mean they'll be like that for the rest of their lives. In fact, what seems like a mess to you might bring your child comfort. Sometimes a messy room is a misguided effort at liberation. It could mean *"I don't like the way I look, so I try on 25 different outfits and I don't have time to put them away before school."* Of course, sometimes a child simply may not be as neat as their parents are.

**What you can do**

To let your child know you'd like for them to clean up their space, try to present your thoughts/questions in a non-critical tone. "What can I do to help you keep your room clean? Do you need more storage space? Do you have clothes that you cannot wear any longer that we could give to charity?" If they are having a difficult time with organization or sorting their items, try to work together to develop a system for putting papers, books, their cell phone and such where they can easily find them. If your child needs more privacy, consider giving it to them, if they are clear about not doing things that are off-limits, like snapchatting instead of doing homework, or surfing inappropriate websites. It may not be your dream scenario but giving your child space to become themselves is a safe way for them to express themselves and explore their personality. Try to compromise if possible: Once a week, they do their laundry and pick up items off the floor of their bedroom. The rest of the time, you let them be—and close the door to their room if you need that for your own sanity.


**Athletic: The child who wants to be like LeBron or Tom Brady**

**vs.**

**the parent who cannot ride a bike without falling and breaking a leg (literally)**

**What you need to know**

It doesn't matter if you enjoy sporting events or not, what matters is the love that you have for your child and the desire to learn about his/her world. Letting our children teach us about the things they are passionate about helps us connect with them and comprehend what is important in their lives.

**What you can do**

Try to never imply or say that you are not interested in sports or express frustration with the sport that your child chooses to try. Your child will view that as something that you do not agree with or something that you put down. Instead, try to let them know that although the sport that they chose may not your area of strength, but that you are excited that they are choosing a new sport and that possibly you could learn about it together. Look into opportunities at school or in your community for them to play/practice their sport of choice, and attend their practices and games. Ask your child questions that allow him/her to be the expert and to be able to teach you. It will give them a sense of mastery and self-confidence. For example: "Why do you like scoring goals as opposed to being the goalie and saving them?" Use their interest in sports to get both of you moving. Practicing shooting soccer goals together. Ask them, "Will you show me how to properly kick the ball into the goal? I can't do it." Modeling *not* being good at something is a fabulous opportunity for your child to see you not as an expert in something. It also allows your child be the expert and gives them permission not to be good at something, too.

## Non-social: The child who would rather camouflage themselves into the wall
### vs.
### The social-butterfly / busy-body (as my husband calls me) parent.

**What you need to know**

Although your child's inhibition may concern you because you love to socialize, it's only problematic if it's a problem for your child. Spending time alone may mean that he/she enjoys their own company, which is a sign of solid self-esteem. Your child may also like things quieter and less hectic. Talk to your child and their teacher to determine how they are interacting socially at school; it could be that they are just careful and take their time to make friends a characteristic you may want to encourage.

**What you can do**

Rather than trying to make your "shy" child outgoing—which would be in contrast to their nature and may make them feel like something is wrong with them —work from their strengths. Your child may not be quick to warm up to new individuals, but are they observant? Do they seem to assess the situation and their peers before they plunge into friendships? Point out what they do that does work: "I love how you took your time to get to know Anita before you felt comfortable going over to her house. The way that you handled that showed really good thinking!" "I could tell that you didn't feel comfortable with Aunt Ida, and it's okay that you didn't want to hug her. I'm glad you did what you thought was best. You should always do that!'" Role-play ways to meet new people that allow your child to stay in her comfort zone without seeming rude, and do it in baby steps. For instance, instead of saying, "Say hello to Cousin Devin, look him in the eye, and shake his hand," which could be overwhelming, you may want to instead say, "I know that it may be hard for you to say hello and to look Cousin Devin in the eye, but good manners are a way we respect people. If you don't want to speak, you could smile and wave to him from a safe distance." Then have them practice with you. And try to avoid calling your child "shy" when talking to them or to others in front of them. Your child is who they are, and that's fine without labeling their traits. If you're worried that your child isn't socializing enough with peers, ask them if there's someone they would like to invite over to play or meet at the park and play with. Don't pressure them to try to be the most popular kid in the class; they may be the kind of person who is happy with their one friend who is their neighbor instead of their classmate. If you feel that it is necessary for them to be more popular, that may be your issue, not theirs.

**Non-Studious: the child that hates going to school and you must drag out of bed every morning**

**vs.**

**The parent who has always loved school and all things academic and lets everyone know it**

### What you need to know

While striving for academic excellence is vital, straight A's and 4.0's are not crucial to future achievement. What you as a parent need to assess, however, is whether your child is trying their absolute best and still not getting A's or whether they are slacking off because of not understanding, a learning difference or just needing a different boost. Putting good grades aside, if your child is really trying, their work ethic will benefit them in the long run. Children who believe that they do well on tests because they work hard actually challenge themselves more than those who think they ace tests because they're naturally smart, according to studies from Stanford University. What's important is to help your child find his/her passion and work toward that. What children need to learn is that education and effort are important; it's okay to ask for help if they need it; and if they're working hard and the best they can do is a B, that's great. Many successful people got B's in school. (Written by someone who thinks they turned out OK).

**What you can do**

Take time to problem-solve with your child. If they are making courageous efforts and still not understanding the material, decide with them if they would like to have a tutor for extra assistance, or see if one of their teachers can offer extra help after or before school. If you are suspicious that your child isn't doing the work or putting forth the effort, have a conversation with them and say something like, "How can I help you be more accountable about your schoolwork? Let's come up with ideas together." Support their love of learning and avoid comparisons if they are less successful in some subjects than others. Try to provide a structure and foundation for success that includes a designated time and place for homework, limited phone and screen time and an absence of video games during the school week. It is always best if the child's motivation can be intrinsic, so attempt to nurture their genuine intellectual curiosity, even if it's a narrow or idiosyncratic interest like saving the ocelots. Your child can read and expand their learning skills while exploring almost any topic. Granted the subject may bore you to tears, show interest in it anyways, and let your child teach you what they know. It will encourage them to want to keep learning. Above all else, remember that your child is a different student than you were, and they learn differently than you probably did. Do not pressure them to get the grades you did or compare them to what you were like in school at their age. Children of high-achieving parents can struggle to feel a sense of their own accomplishment.

## Creative: The right-brain, unicorn child

## vs.

## The left brain, I-hate-all-craft-stores parent

**What you need to know**

You do not have to be decent at creating art in order to appreciate it, especially one of your own child's creations. Your young DaVinci's masterpiece can give you some perception into your child's mind. Creating something with your child is a wonderful opportunity to have fun together and for both of you relax and get your fingers dirty.

**What you can do**

When your child brings one of their MANY art creations home from school, ask them specific questions about it. "How did you figure out that you wanted to draw something like this? How did you make the hair look like that?" "Why did you color the person in the picture blue and orange?" Answers to these kinds of questions can give you peeks into your child's thinking. If they say, "I colored my person blue because I was sad that day and then when I got happy again I was orange!" you're learning something about how they feel." These types of conversations can help to begin a deeper conversation with your child about why they were sad and then what made them feel better. Take time to speak to the art teacher at school about your child's potential and how you can encourage it—perhaps by providing the right materials and the time to create more at home. Visit museums with your children; read books or watch programs about artists and interesting art pieces together. Some parents may worry that encouraging a talented young artist may send them down the starving artist career path. Eventually, you need to permit your child to follow his/her passions regardless of what they are. They will become what they will become and at the end of the day, it's not up to you. Whether your kids share traits with you, your spouse/partner, or neither, all kids are individuals with astounding interests and abilities. To compartmentalize them as being "just like us" or "like nobody I know" may limit their potential to develop into unique adults. One of the great joys of parenting is seeing life through your child's eyes. The more different they are from you, the fresher that viewpoint. Take time to get to know, appreciate and understand their personality and you will not only see the world in a new way, you will be able to see something even more thrilling: how your child fits into it.

Review the questions below and answer them as honestly as you can. There are no right or wrong answers.

1. ***Do I lead my children more than I manage them?***

Note: Parenting is a primarily a role of authority and leadership. Leading requires a vision and a plan—and there is no better place to start than the wide perspective of this space. Leading is knowing *who* you want to be as a parent and *where* you want your family to be in the future, arising from a powerful *why*. Leading is knowing who your children are, their unique personalities and strengths.

Management is in the structure and systems of the day-to-day and is meaningless and chaotic without a healthy relationship, a sense of purpose, and a plan. The more you lead and the clearer you are about where you are heading, the less you will manage.

If you find yourself constantly managing, reacting or punishing, then it's time to step back and ask: Why am I getting more of the same each day?

## 2. What did I take from my own experience of being parented?

One of the most important research findings is that a robust predictor of parenting behaviors is whether they have made sense of their own experience of being parented. It is liberating to know that regardless of where you fall on the continuum of these childhood experiences, the most important factor is whether or not your narrative is coherent. When you have made sense of your childhood and the way your parents raised you, you are emotionally free to be present. The past does not intrude upon the present and you can truly be with your children.

### 3. Do my parenting actions flow from thought-out principles and values?

While we may have to sort through many thoughts and feelings, our choices in the moment are critical and reflect an underlying belief system. This may be the parenting style you experienced as a child, or what the culture says about parenting. Regardless, every parent has a belief system, whether it is conscious or not.

While some parents have professed a "Because I said so" stance, every action we take or choice we make speaks of a quality that we wish for in our children. These qualities are the intangibles that make up character, such as responsibility, respect, and integrity. Notably, research points to a lack of self-regulation in children who are parented in an authoritarian style ("Because I said so"). The same is true for a permissive style featuring a lack of appropriate limit-setting and consequences.

### 4. Do I set limits and boundaries effectively for my children?

Most parents come into the role being better at one of the two main functions: Either they feel more comfortable with the nurturing and supporting aspect of the role or the discipline and management side. Regardless, we as parents need to be adept in both functions through each developmental stage. One of the key aspects of discipline is setting limits. For those who struggle with limit-setting, it is hard to say "no," set boundaries or hold a child accountable. The child's feeling of disappointment or his/her pushback may be hard for a parent to manage emotionally and either they give in or sidestep the limit. But the most important principle is that limits help children to feel safe and, when properly set, are inherently loving. Over time, limits teach children what is limitless within. Additionally, setting a limit does not necessarily mean that what is beyond the limit is bad or unhealthy. You can't say "yes" to everything, otherwise nothing has any meaning or value.

### 5. Have I built a balanced social and emotional life for each relationship with my family?

Relationships with your children are dynamic and require consistent attention. Importantly, attention to each individual within the family is important to development and a healthy sense of self. Within a family the individual is part of a unit and plays a role. Taking the time to connect, listen, be with, and share experiences builds trust as we adapt to each other. Consistent routines and scheduling time for relationship-building helps with this process both on the individual and family level.

**6. Do I know the strengths, interests, and exceptional qualities in each of my children?**

Seeing a child for who they are sends a powerful message to them. Nurturing and supporting the unique characteristics of personality and abilities communicates acceptance and provides a mirror for children to see who they are and what they can become. Here, fairness is treating children differently based on their unique needs.

## 7. Do I nurture autonomy, cooperation, and curiosity in each of my children on a daily basis?

This question connects to leading and a long-term perspective founded in the basic needs of being human. A major aspect of a healthy attachment is providing a secure home base for a child to feel confident to explore. While children are dependent, we need to nurture independence and creativity through guidance, choice, and a stimulating environment. Modeling and coaching the interpersonal skills of getting along, listening, and delaying gratification will go a long way in helping children to develop a cooperative nature in social settings.

## 8. Am I growing as a parent?

Missing in many theories of parenting is the arc of adult development. While stages of child development have been explained, the world of parenting is presented as a flat surface - where content, skills, and information are added to a fixed parenting mindset. Personal development does not end in adulthood or parenthood, but unlike the arc of child development, growth does become a choice.

# Chapter 5

# Healthy Boundaries & Relationships

*"Think of a boundary as the line you draw around yourself to define where you end and where your child begins." Debbie Pincus, MS LMHC*

As parents it is your responsibility to set specific limits and make clear the repercussions if those limits are exceeded. Children need to know what the limits are. They are basically asking the question, *"Who is in charge and who makes the rules in our family?"* They need to know that it is not them – that is too big a burden! The rules should be expressed clearly and consistently. Rules can be simple, like: you shouldn't hurt others, you shouldn't hurt things, you shouldn't hurt yourself. Consistently repeat the rules and include the reason behind them. For instance, "Legos are for building with. If we bang them on the table, it could break. Let's build a tower." Swoop and scoop a toddler who is heading for the stove that is turned on. "Appliances that have heat can be dangerous. No touching!"

A young child feels abandoned when his parents give up setting boundaries and say things like, "There's nothing we can do to stop him. If we say 'no' to more candy, he just helps himself." If the rule is that he may only take one piece of candy, then you must enforce the boundary. A fantastic way to phrase a boundary is, "In our family we...". This establishes a family rule that includes every member.

**Guidelines for Creating Successful Parent-Child Relationships**

- ☐ Try to set aside time on a regular basis to do something fun with your child.
- ☐ Try to not disagree about discipline with your partner in front of the children.
- ☐ Never give an order, request, or command without being able to enforce it at the time.
- ☐ Be consistent, that is, reward or punish the same behavior in the same manner as much as possible.
- ☐ Agree on what behavior is desirable and not desirable.
- ☐ Agree on how to respond to undesirable behavior.

- ☐ Make it as clear as possible what the child is to expect if he or she performs the undesirable behavior.
- ☐ Make it very clear what the undesirable behavior is. It is not enough to say, "Your room is messy." Messy should be specified in terms of exactly what is meant: "You've left dirty clothes on the floor, dirty plates on your desk, and your bed is not made."
- ☐ Once you have stated your position and the child attempts to argue, do not keep defending your position. Just restate your position once more and then stop responding to the comments.
- ☐ Look for gradual changes in behavior. Don't expect too much.
- ☐ Praise behavior that is coming closer to the desired goal.
- ☐ Remember that your behavior serves as a model for your children's behavior.
- ☐ If one parent is disciplining a child and the other enters the room, that other person should not step in on the argument in progress.
- ☐ Reward desirable behavior as much as possible by verbal praise or touch. Do not always reward behavior with something tangible such as a toy, food or money.
- ☐ Both parents should have an equal share in the responsibility of discipline as much as possible.
- ☐ Demonstrate in detail how you would like children to behave. Have them practice the behavior. Give them

encouragement along with constructive criticism.
- ☐ Try to set aside time on a regular basis to do something fun with your children.
- ☐ Rather than tell them what not to do, teach and show them what they should do.
- ☐ Use descriptive praise when they do something well. Say, "I like how you ____ when you ____." Be specific.
- ☐ Help your child learn to express how they feel. Say: "You seem frustrated." "How are you feeling?" "Are you upset?" "You look like you are angry about that." "It's OK to feel that way."
- ☐ Try to see a situation the way your children do. Listen carefully to them. Try to form a mental picture of how it would look to them.
- ☐ Use a soft, confident tone of voice to redirect them when they are upset.
- ☐ Be a good listener. Use good eye contact. Physically get down to the level of smaller children. Don't interrupt. Ask open-ended questions rather than questions that can be answered with a yes or no. Repeat back to them what you heard.
- ☐ Make sure children understand directions. Have them repeat them back.
- ☐ When possible give children choices of when and how to comply with a request.
- ☐ Look for gradual changes in behavior. Don't expect too much. Praise behavior that is coming closer to

the desired goal.
- ☐ Develop a nonverbal sign (gesture) that your children will accept as a signal that they are being inappropriate and need to change their behavior. This helps them to respond to your prompt without getting upset.

- **What is meaningful to YOUR child/tween/teen? (may not be the same as your friend's child!)**

- **Are you prepared to follow through every time (at least at first)?**

- **Timing – you may want to start at a time that's more relaxed and not when you must get out the door for work.**

- **How do you want to talk with your child/adolescent about it?**

# Chapter 6

# Communicating with Your Children

When my kids were younger, I would always ask them about their "rose" of the day and their "thorn" of their day. This was a fair way for them to discuss (without one person hogging all the airtime at the dinner table) the things that mattered to them the most in their day. It allowed me as a parent to establish a meaningful daily tradition that each member of the family looked forward to. It gave my kids a guide map and starter for conversations that they may or may not have wanted to have with me or the entire family. It also helped them to remember certain meaningful parts of their day. They ended up jumping into the car at the end of a school day ready to declare their "rose" and "thorn" for the day.

In this section, we provide tools for enriching and strengthening conversations with your children. One great way to encourage children to open up is to make a habit of cherishing daily conversations with your child. Conversations build connection. When children feel connected to their parent, they are more likely to feel well and be cooperative. When we pause and listen, we can really get to know so much about our children. Sometimes our children don't readily open up and share about their day. It can be frustrating when all you want is to talk to your child and you are met with a frown and heavy sighs. Ever felt like you don't know what to ask to get a child to open up?

Most parents really do want to know about their child's thoughts, dreams and concerns. To raise resilient, happy children, it's important to listen to our children often. Being invited into the child's world allows us to be helpful and supportive parents. The million dollar question is, *so how to get kids talking?* The more our children feel they can talk to us about the little things, the more likely they will be to open about the bigger issues later on. We give our children an amazing gift by simply being present when they talk to us. When we hold judgement and listen to our children with the intent to discover, support and connect, magic happens!

The most effective way of communicating is to use your voice well. Calm and confident – bright with expectation of compliance. When you yell and scream, you are communicating that you are losing control. This brings about non-compliance in children.

**How to discuss things with your child:**

- Be near your child and able to touch him (not ten feet or a full room away).
- Look at your child and smile.
- Use as pleasant a voice tone as possible.
- Make sure your child is facing you and looking at you.
- Praise your child. "Hey that's great. You're really doing a nice job. That's really helping me." Reward your child with your appreciation. "Thank you for doing a great job."
- Describe the appropriate behavior for your child so that they will know exactly what behavior he/she is being praised and rewarded for.
- Hug your child occasionally or use some other form of positive touch.
- Have your child acknowledge you, such as, "Thanks, Mom" or "O.K."

**Things to try**:
**Say yes**

Often you must refuse a child's request, but you will engage cooperation much more if you can put a positive spin on it. "Yes, when…" is much better than, "No!"

**Spend time together**

There are times to park and sit with your child away from an activity. Your presence is comforting. Your stillness allows them to think. Your invitation to try again tells them you believe in them.

**Follow through on what you say**

There are also times to show direct firmness. Your child has thrown the toy and damaged the wall. You should take the toy and quietly put it away. Do not argue. It is not up for discussion. Follow through on what the consequences are.

We have developed a series of conversation starters you can use, organized by age. The conversation starters were designed to make it especially hard for your child to reply with one-word answers! Try these out with your children.

*Elementary School (Ages 5-10) Favorites*

*Who is your best friend?*

*What is your favorite subject in school?*

*Who is your favorite superhero?*

*Who is your favorite teacher?*

*If you could be a character from a book, who would you be?*

*Add in your own questions here.*

_____
_____
_____
_____
_____
_____

The No-Fuss Simple Approach to Parenting

*Middle School (Ages 10-14) Favorites*

*Who is your favorite musical artist?*

*What is your favorite book?*

*What is your favorite thing to do with your friends?*

*Who is your personal hero?*

*Who are your favorite teachers?*

*If you could design a t-shirt, what would you draw or write on it?*

*Add your personal questions here:*

_____
_____
_____

_____
_____
_____


*High School (Ages 14-18) Favorites*

*How would you describe your perfect day?*

*If you could change one thing in the world, what would it be?*

*What do you like most about yourself?*

*What qualities do you value most in a friend?*

*What is your biggest dream?*

_____
_____
_____

_____
_____
_____

# Chapter 7

# Understanding Your Child's Cues

The truth is, no matter how prepared you are in parenting, you will still face challenges as your child grows through different phases of their life. Watching my children struggle without stepping in to fix things for them was always one of the hardest parenting challenges I experienced as a mom, even though I knew it was the best thing for both of my children. Being a parent is a balance of taking care of your kids while letting them grow up and learn from their mistakes. Your role of simply loving and protecting your child from pain and uneasiness changes to one of accepting that your child (no matter how old they are) will need to experience natural consequences for his or her actions. The hard part—for them and for us—is that each consequence almost always include some distress, embarrassment, disappointment, and agony.

Understanding your child's social and emotional cues can help you be responsive to their individual needs. All humans can communicate without speaking. This is called nonverbal communication—gestures, facial expressions or postures that communicate feelings. If you are in dialogue with someone and they have their back turned to you and they are looking at their cell phone, they are using their non-verbal communication skills to let you know that they either are bored, or they want to you to stop talking to them. Without having to use any words, they are letting us know what they need or want.

As parents, we continuously strive for our children to be successful, to be happy, and to behave and participate in day to day activities with their peers and family members. Sometimes, it's much easier said than done. We wonder why our toddler throws temper tantrums, why our babies cry for what we think is no reason, or why our teenagers pretend we don't exist. Behavior and understanding your child's social cues can be such a mystery for parents as well as cause many parents stress and anxiety! We then ask ourselves, "Why isn't our child *normal?*"

The truth of the matter is there is no "normal" anything in relation to the children that we are raising. When you feel confused about the way your child behaves, it is imperative not to panic, and to remain as calm as possible. It is essential for parents to comprehend that all behavior has meaning. Babies, young children and teenagers consistently send the adults in their lives, nonverbal communication cues all the time. A baby cries when they are hungry or wet because they can't tell you what they need with words. A toddler might grab your hand and lead you to the kitchen to tell you they are hungry or hide behind you at a family reunion to say they are overwhelmed. A teenager may go into the kitchen and stare intently into the open refrigerator doors, indicating that they are "starving" and looking for food. As parents, when we take the time to pay attention to, recognize, and understand our child's perspective, we can also better understand their behaviors. Understanding why a child is doing something makes it easier to react to them in a way that is responsive to their needs.

**Think about the "why?"** When your child does something or has a certain inflection in their voice, take the time to think about why they might be doing it that way. What are they trying to communicate to you? Do they need something from you to meet their needs?

**Respond, don't react.** Instead of immediately reacting with your own emotions to your child's actions, try to take a minute to process how to respond to your child. You might want to scream and immediately discipline your child when they write on the wall with a crayon, but if you take a minute to process, you can respond calmly and address their needs.

**Make sure your child's primary needs are met.** Sometimes children misbehave or have strong emotional outbursts when their primary needs aren't met. As a parent, you can be responsive to your child by making sure they have what they need to be happy and successful. Are they getting enough to eat? Are they sleepy? Did they have the appropriate number of hours of rest and downtime that they need to be successful throughout the day? Have they had enough physical interaction from you or other family members? Have they gotten enough hugs, kisses and attention?

**Be responsive.** Sometimes it is easier to take a "one-size-fits-all" solution to solving problems with young children. For example, sending a child to time-out anytime they have broken a rule. It is much more effective to respond to your child's specific cues or needs. When your child draws on the wall they might be telling you they are bored and need help to release their energy in a productive way. Modify your response to your child's behavior in order to fit their specific needs.

When you respond to your child's social and emotional cues, your children will feel loved, understood and less frustrated. Tune in to your child's social and emotional cues, be calm and responsive and you can build a strong and compassionate relationship with your child.

**Help your child – how can you work together to make this better next time?**

You cannot always understand what your child is trying to communicate. But remember:

- You can always try again. When you respond to your child, say out loud what you think his/her behavior might mean, in a calm, positive manner. For example, you might say to the toddler you pick up, "Are you saying that you want up? I can pick you up." By using language to describe what your child is communicating, you will be teaching them the meaning of words and helping them learn to share their emotions.

- Look at each situation as an opportunity to learn more about your child and how they think as individuals or when dealing with a stressful situation – what do you know now that you didn't know about your child prior to this situation?

- What tools or resources may your child need in the future?

- Teach your child how they may behave, act, or react differently in the future. Children do not always know how to behave appropriately. Model suitable behavior and language for your child throughout daily activities and routines.

It is important for parents to understand their child's social and emotional cues, and not avoid situations that may be frustrating. The more you try to understand, help, and teach your child, the more their conduct will improve. Parents face many challenges. And as we all find out, there are many, many challenges that we never expected or knew about before having children! As a mom and educator of over 18 years, I've found the following to be five of the most difficult.

**1. Parenting the child you have and not the child you wish you had.**

Often, we try to parent our kids based on who we think they should be instead of who they really are. Listen, it can be tough and exhausting to have a son with ADHD or a teen with ODD who's defiant and disrespectful. Or you might have a child who's very different from you. So, trying to see their side of things becomes a constant, draining battle. You might think, "Hey, this isn't what I signed up for! Is this what parenthood is supposed to be like?" As a mom and educator, I know that when you accept that your child is not who you thought they were going to be, real anguish can emerge. You might have to give up certain dreams you had for your child's future when you realize she is not going to take the path you'd hoped she would.

Understand, though, that once you let go and accept who your child is, a different kind of love can develop. You'll be able to see them clearly for the person that they truly are. I have found that true acceptance is one of the most powerful, loving things a parent can give to their child. It's the basis for so many things, including being able to develop and communicate reasonable expectations for appropriate behavior. Old power struggles fall away, which can give you space to nurture new aspects of your relationship. And as an added bonus, when you accept your child for who they are, they can then become better at accepting themselves.

## 2. Letting your child experience the pain and discomfort of natural consequences.

In general, it's not a good idea to try to protect your child from experiencing the consequences of their actions. How will your child learn from his poor choices if you take away the natural consequences of those choices? We humans learn through trial and error. It is often the best way to learn. We speed. We get a ticket. And we eventually stop speeding.

Your child cannot learn if you put up a protective fence around them and try to fix things for them. As my a former colleague of mine often says, "It's helpful to allow your child to struggle. Change happens out of struggle and in moments of accepting responsibility for our actions."

It's our job as parents to help our kids through these difficult times, but it's not our job to bear all their burdens for them. This may mean letting your child feel some pain and the disappointment of natural consequences if they have acted out. You can help them by talking to them about how they can handle themselves differently next time and teaching them some good coping strategies. By simply letting your children know you're there for them because you love them, you are giving them one of the most important things a parent can ever give.

**3. Dealing with judgment, shame, and blame from others.**

If you have a child who acts out and engages in other challenging behaviors—tantrums, yelling, disobeying you or being annoying and obnoxious—you have probably gotten "the look" from friends and strangers. You know the one—it says, "What's wrong with you? Why are you allowing your child to behave that way?" It can make you feel like a terrible parent, even if you know you're doing everything you can to raise your child the best you know how. And the truth is, others will probably judge you—it's human nature. If you are in this situation, it's natural to worry about your child disappointing you or embarrassing you. It is also natural to worry about how others will react to your child's misbehavior and then blame you.

When your child is acting out and you're feeling judged by others, stop and say to yourself, "I can't read other people's minds." If you try to imagine what others are thinking, 95 percent of the time you're going to guess something negative. That's because whenever we're negative, we interpret other people's perceptions of us as negative, too. And in these situations, we don't read people's minds in search of hope. We read them in search of criticism—especially when something is going wrong.

So, when you feel yourself trying to guess what another parent in your child's class, your mother-in-law or your friends are thinking, just tell yourself, "I'm not a mind-reader; I don't know what they're thinking." Stop the tape that's playing in your head and move on. This is also part of the process of learning how to engage in "positive self-talk," or talking to yourself in a way that promotes calmness and hope, rather than panic.

**4. "I hate you!"**

The words "I hate you" or "you are horrible" can have the power to reduce any parent to tears or anger. It can make you feel like you've failed and wonder where you went wrong. One of the hardest things that parents face is when their child is mean, rude, or disrespectful. Your child may have always been this way. Or the change in their personality might have seemingly happened overnight—perhaps when they hit the pre-teen years. One day your ten-year-old loves being with you. The next day she's screaming "I hate you," calling you names and refusing to go anywhere with you.

Children know that saying these words can paralyze a parent during a fight, which is why they use this tactic to get what they want. As hard as it is, try not to personalize your child's behavior, even when they say that they hate you. When you personalize things, it makes it very hard to be objective about how to respond to your child in the moment. A good thing to do when this happens is stop, breathe, and instead of a knee-jerk reaction, respond with something like the following:

> *"We're not talking about that right now. We're talking about the fact that you need to do your homework."*

You can also ask yourself, "What does my child really need from me *right now*?" It might be some space. Or it might be for you to follow through on a consequence you issued. But remember, try not to take these words from your kids personally.

**5. Letting go.**

During your child's pre-adolescent and adolescent years, you are constantly confronted with the challenge of letting go. This is especially difficult if your kid seems to need to learn things the hard way. A natural part of adolescence is risk-taking — which often results in breaking rules and inappropriate behavior. It becomes extremely important as a parent to be able to disconnect from your own emotional response to this misbehavior.

Emotional responses include feeling guilty, embarrassed, ashamed, or disappointed. As parents, when our kids get older, we need to pull back a bit and become coaches and teachers while we let our kids begin to play the game of life. We still love our children as people, but we give them space to learn, space for trial and error. As painful as it is to accept sometimes, our children are born to move away from us. There is a sense of grief that goes along with this. I've experienced it myself. It's important to remember that this work of caring for our children while they are constantly separating from us and becoming individuals can be stressful, demanding, and confusing.

**Be a "good enough" parent.**

It's difficult for parents to figure out what is right, and the truth is, there really isn't a "right" answer all the time. It's important to accept that there are choices to make and that choices often come with anxiety. Remember that you are doing the best you can and that you won't be perfect. More important than trying to be a perfect parent is to be a "good enough" parent. A "good enough" takes care of their child and tries their best. Hard situations are part of life – but these situations can help us learn and grow. You can't protect your children from everything bad that might happen to them. Or from the poor choices they may make. But you can help them learn from the bad situations they get themselves into. Your child will likely not thank you now for letting them struggle on their own and suffer through a consequence, but they may surprise you when they become an adult by telling you that your coaching, teaching or limit setting made a positive difference in their life. This is "good enough."

# Chapter 8

# The ABC's of Discipline

When my kids were little, I decorated a wooden spoon. Her name was "Miss Act Right!" I glued on googly eyes and drew a face complete with make-up. I added yarn for hair and she was complete. "Miss Act Right" was to serve as a reminder for my children to be on their best behavior. For my son, the oldest by 2.5 years, all it took was a glance at "Miss Act Right." All I had to do was stand her up in my purse so that he could get a visual. That is all that it took. He knew immediately what she stood for and that he needed to straighten his behavior up. For my daughter, the baby, the strong-willed child – Miss Act Right was just a silly dressed up spoon, a visual that did nothing to tame her behavior or thought pattern.

Whether you are raising a toddler or a teenager, there will always be some form of discipline you will need to have in place. Children come on board most readily when they have had some input into the rule-making. Discipline and boundaries should never be a surprise for your child. They shouldn't suddenly discover they have transgressed some rule or made you angry without knowing it. Your expectations should be clearly expressed.

Most pediatricians, educators and social workers agree that consistency is key for all preschoolers for effective disciplining. When the routine is not consistent, preschoolers get confused and may act out more or throw more temper tantrums. It is easy to focus on your child's negative actions, like yelling and screaming, and ignore the good more acceptable behaviors. Instead notice the good behaviors and give attention to those things. Consistently provide instruction, discipline, praise, or appreciation for your child as the situation warrants. When you issue a punishment stick to it, and make sure your child abides by it. They do not avoid doing these things because they are tired, overwhelmed with other life commitments, or are finding it difficult to see the point in the moment.

**Guidelines for Discipline**
- Hold to the same principles and practices.

- Plan ahead of time

- Calm, consistent, decisive, fair

- Link logical consequences to the child's behavior whenever possible

For good behaviors:
- Reward talking nicely with extra phone time
- Reward homework completion with extra free time

**For not OK behavior:**
If your child is acting up to get out of something, it's important that the consistent consequence doesn't help them to get out of it, accidentally!

## Be consistent, honest, fair, and firm as you relate to your child.

Most behaviors have a reason behind them- they are reactions. Your child may be acting out to get something they want, to get out of something they don't want, for safety/security or power/control/influence. For most "not OK" behaviors, the reason is understandable, even if the behavior is not. Try your best to understand what's causing the behavior.

Once you identify the problem next decide how you will deal with it. If the behavior is complicated (lots of parts), pick one part that you think you could address. For example, your child rarely does the chores and gives you an 'attitude' when you ask. Pick either doing the chore or addressing the attitude (hint, picking the chore might be an easier place to start!). Next give clear and concise instructions and determine the timing. Does this need to be made now? How important is it? Is it necessary for the running of the household?. From there you will need to address your proximity – am I close to my child/adolescent when I give the instruction?

When it comes to behavior the language you use or don't use is important. Evaluate your language before you address the situation. Use your "Do" language – does the instruction tell my child/tween/teen what **to do** (as opposed to what not to do). Be clear. Is the instruction succinct? Avoid (when possible) asking as a question, giving too many instructions or giving vague instructions.

| Behavior | Parent Reaction / Action |
| --- | --- |
| Talking back | Show interest when child is talking respectfully. |
| | Have a conversation about at neutral time about ground/house rules. |
| | If the time is right, have the conversation about ground house rules. |
| | Model talking respectfully. |

| Whining/Hitting | Make sure instructions are well timed. |
| --- | --- |
| | Get close to child, within arm's reach. |
| | Make eye contact. |
| | Give clear instructions with a calm voice. |
| Messy room | Address one item to put away at a time |
| Emotional outburst | Go to room to calm down when upset |

**Guidelines for Parents When Disciplining Your Child**
- ☐ Be near you child and able to touch him/her.
- ☐ Use a pleasant voice tone if possible.
- ☐ Make sure your child is facing you and looking at you.
- ☐ Explain what was inappropriate such as, "Remember you are not allowed to run in the kitchen because it is not safe." "You need to learn not to lower your voice in the house so that we can enjoy being together at home and not disturb any family members who are trying to concentrate on other things."
- ☐ Be sympathetic. "I know it's hard to not jump on the bed but that's the rule."
- ☐ Give your child the consequence.
- ☐ Make sure your child gets the appropriate consequence.
- ☐ If your child is too mad or upset to discuss the issue, don't force it. Place your child in time out (to cool off) and then discuss later.

**1. Is the discipline that I gave my child somehow related to the child's behavior? "Does the fine fit the crime?"**

It is always important that the discipline matches up with the action. This will help the child understand logical consequences and learn the intended lesson more clearly. For example, if your child makes a bad choice playing outside with friends, he shouldn't be able to play outside the next day. You can use our Socially Wize Consequence Guide to come up with your own plan for effective discipline.

**2. Does this teach my child what they need to do differently?**

I have seen many parents scold their child for making a bad choice, but not actually take the time to tell their child WHY what they did was not OK. It is important that you take the time to teach your child about the problem AND share with them what you expect from them moving forward. For example, if a child is jumping off the swing at the playground, don't just say "No." Explain to her/him how that is a dangerous choice and they could be giving a negative example to younger kids at the park. Talk to them about the appropriate way to play safely on the playground.

**3. Is my child's negative behavior changing?**

Many parents experience the feeling that nothing is working to change a behavior. If you find yourself at this point, this could mean that you need to try some new strategies to get the results that you are looking for.

**4. Does the discipline create a connection or disconnection between my child and me?**

It is important that your child knows you are the parent, but also still feels and accepts your love afterwards. The way you act and communicate that the behavior is not okay can make a big difference. If you are yelling, critical, or aggressive, your child may feel that the relationship is distant after the incident.

**5. Does the discipline fit my child?**

Each child has unique needs and personalities, which means you need to look at the child to make sure it matches. Different ages and developmental abilities are important to consider.

**6. Did my child learn how to "own" what happened and take responsibility?**

It is important for your child to accept his part in the incident and not blame everyone else. You want your child to really understand that they had a choice and that he/she needs to make a different choice next time.

**7. Did I separate who my child is from what my child did?**

You want your child to know that just because they made

a bad choice, they are not a bad child for doing so. Focus on the behavior being bad– and not the child. This helps the child maintain self-esteem and not feel ashamed.

**8. Can I honestly follow through easily and sustain this?**

It's important to make sure that whatever technique you choose for disciplining your child is something you can keep up with and follow through on. You may have many great ideas, but if it's not a good match for you to maintain them then you may need to explore some simpler options. Being consistent and following through are key ways to maintain good boundaries with your children.

# Chapter 9

# Teach Your Child Responsibility

You can't really talk about independence without talking about responsibility. In my experience I have noticed, most parents have a tough time teaching their children to be more responsible. At Socially Wize we believe you can start giving age-appropriate responsibilities to kids as young as five or six. Your child should have to earn independence by being able to handle responsibility. An example might be an expectation that your first grader will get ready for school in the morning and begin to take care of his room a little. You will need to help him/her at this young age by taking on the teacher and coach roles. Remember, you're a role model for your child and you're also encouraging and supporting him when he gets it right. It goes without saying that middle and high school students should be actively participating in the responsibilities around the home. They may be resistant and will probably argue with you over every request, enforce this anyways. Most of the teens I worked with in underserved areas had little or no experience with appropriate responsibility. By the time they left my program, they would often say to me, "I really disliked you at first, but you made me do things I'd never done before. You were tough, but you helped me to change and to grow up." I think that's just how it feels sometimes for kids. Most of the time, they're not happy with you for asking them to do things. But when they reach adulthood, they usually understand that this is how you've helped them grow up.

In my experience, yelling and screaming at my children and or students really didn't accomplish much. If you're nagging your child over a task all the time, it's probably the wrong task. In other words, give realistic responsibility towards realistic independence. One example is parents who buy pets for children. Realistically, most kids are not going to be able to take on the full responsibility of managing a pet. A younger child is not going to be capable of it and adolescents do not always have the focus to take that all on. Some pieces should be taken on by your child, but other pieces are probably going to fall to you, more like a co-responsibility.

**Take an Analysis**

Look at how important the task is in your child's life. Is it a skill they need to acquire at that point in time? Is it something that may have consequences if they fail to do it? If they don't get up for school and they miss a class, it's going to create problems in school and their grades might be affected. Other things, like making the bed every day, may not be as important and may not have huge consequences.

Either way, make sure, whether it's a task of responsibility or a task of independence, that your child has the best chance to succeed. The goal is to coach, teach and support your kids in gaining independence so they can become independent, responsible adults. It may seem obvious to you how to load the dishwasher. But your child may need to be taught what goes where. By teaching him to do it, you're giving him the chance to succeed.

It is my opinion parents need to take it step by step and be reasonable with their goal setting. Expecting perfection from kids who take on new responsibilities is probably not going to work. Be realistic and pick and choose what you're going to battle over, if anything. And remember, you can always back down. Just because you've set something up, you can step back from it and reset your expectations if it's not working. And always start with something smaller and easier; pick something manageable for your child.

If you start when your child is younger, it is much easier for you when they grow older. Then they know what you expect from them and are accustomed to completing the task. Match the building of responsibilities with their age and their actual ability. You're not going to expect an eight-year-old to rake the whole lawn or shovel the driveway by themselves, for example, but you might expect them to come out for half an hour and help you. If your child has a hard time keeping her room clean, you might want to set up areas in the room that have different purposes: a play area, a sleep area and a clothing area. This breaks the chore into smaller, more manageable parts, especially for a younger child.

I always advise parents to step back and assess the situation first. Step away from the argument and talk with your spouse about what's going on. Regroup. Take a good look at what is working with that expectation for your child, and then look at what isn't working.

There are five questions you can ask that will help you as you decide how to handle the situation.

1. What things are important to you as a family? If taking care of pets is important and your child has a role in that, then as a family, that's an important piece. But if no one else makes the bed in the family, for example, it may not be important to expect of that child. This is what I mean by choosing what you're going to do battle over.

2. What things are important to your child and their life? It may not be important to you that your child chooses their own TV programs in the evening. But for your child, it may be important to do that. Or it may be very important for your six-year-old to pick out her own clothes. If these tasks give your child age-appropriate independence, I say let them do it.

3. Does the expectation contribute to the family or household? If your child has a responsibility to empty the dishwasher and that helps the next person who must set the table, that's a more important task than something that doesn't have any connection to anyone else in the family.

4. Can there be some give and take? Can there be a choice to do something similar but different? There may be something your child is more willing or able to do that might be more meaningful to the rest of the family. Remember, the goal is for your child to succeed at what he's doing and to build on that success.

5. Are there things you can do to help organize your child? Can you help structure that task or responsibility so that your child can be more successful? Setting it up so your child can more easily sort the recycling by having a designated area and special bins set up might do wonders to get the job done.

You may need to sit down with your kids and talk about all the things that you have on your plate and how you need them to help. My husband James used to tell our son: "Everyone in the family has a responsibility for the family. Our job is to go to work each day and support the family. Your job is to go to school, learn, come home and contribute to the family." As parents you should be clear with your child about the business aspect of being a family. Chores and school are part of your family's business, and everyone has a job in that business. Phrasing it this way makes it easier for a child of any age to understand.

I know that things are tough for parents right now. There may be situations where one of you lost your job and you're going to need to expect more of your kids than you might have in the past. Or you may be raising a child as a single parent and you're doing the best you can to keep the home together. Depending on your child's age, you can sit down and talk to them about that openly and ask them, "Are there ways you think you might be helpful to the family?" And again, if things don't work, regroup. Re-discuss. Look at your priorities.

When you're giving your child a responsibility to carry out around the house, you might say, "Before you sit down and have your snack when you get home from school, please empty the dishwasher." If you tie it in more logically to other things that your child is doing, he'll be less likely to forget or do something else instead of that task. Some younger kids need visual reminders, such as a chart on the wall with stars.

Other children just need some structure and some consistent expectations. And some kids just need to know that their parents mean it and that they're not going to cave in with the new task or a new responsibility.

If you haven't built in this responsibility over the years, your child may become overly dependent on you. But remember, it's never too late to start. So, if you have a 14-year-old who's never done dishes or made his bed or contributed to the family, you can still begin to teach responsibility now. Don't throw it all at your child at one time; you're still going to have to build up to it. If he's 14 and he's never done anything around the house, he probably doesn't even think he can. You may have to show him how to make his bed or sort the recycling. We assume that kids know how we want things done, and the fact is, they often don't. Even though your child may be older, if he's never done these things before, you still must take it step-by-step and build on skills. Your child must be able to show some success.

If your child refuses to do the chores, the consequence will depend on the task and its importance. If your child is not getting up to go to school, there are going to be consequences. He must be able to go to school. If it's something that's less connected to his success, it may be more effective to find another task that's going to be a little bit more successful.

Most people want to succeed at being responsible, and believe it or not, most kids really do want to be responsible. They don't want to do a lot of work, but they want to feel like they are contributing members of the family. You might have to build that—and I know that with some kids, it's harder than others. Keep that in mind and remember that you might have to teach some basic skills. Without those basic skills, your child may not know how to solve the problem of chores. And besides, aren't teaching and coaching a whole lot less frustrating than nagging and screaming?

**Social Responsibility**

In our world today, there is a focus on self-indulgence. Whether it's clothes, cosmetics, vacations, vehicles or the latest electronic device, marketing departments everywhere are constantly reinforcing the idea that "we're worth it." That's not to say that we can't enjoy our gadgets or our vacations but when there is evidence of need in every city, community and country around the world, it could be considered a little unfair to be so focused on only impacting ourselves.

Teach the joy of giving, not only to family and friends, but to strangers in need. As children we tend to be very aware of the needs of others and are often motivated to help those in need. As we grow older and learn more about the world, we get a little more cynical, a little more self-focused and a little more reluctant to part with our hard-earned cash. Our giving habits, like any other financial habits, is largely influenced by the actions and beliefs of the adults around us as we're growing up. If we want our kids to be generous and empathetic to the needs of others, then we need to give them opportunities to practice giving and we need to give them positive role models to emulate.

It's true that giving doesn't have to be financial; often a donation of time is far more impactful both on the giver and the recipient. However, making it a habit to give money we've earned to benefit causes that matter to us is an important lesson in sharing wealth for kids.

**Children Are Capable of Helping Others**

So how do you inspire a spirit of giving in your kids? Some parents I know choose a charity as a family to support and each family member contributes a portion of their income/allowance. Others regularly volunteer time as a family to fundraise or to support causes that are important to them. However you choose to give, it will be a powerful experience for your kids and if done consistently, is likely to become a lifelong habit. Make allocating money for giving part of your child's savings goals and then give them the freedom to choose where the money goes. Encourage them to give back to their community and to give their time to help others. In our family, we gave both our time and money. Tithing was not an example of giving. That is something that we owe to God. We gave money to specific charities and taught both our son and daughter to do so as well. We spent time creating "blessing bags" to handout to the homeless, we organized clothing and canned foods at shelters and charity/thrift stores. We spent time each month at the community garden, reading to children in shelters, and making holiday food baskets for senior citizens in various communities.

Both my husband and I belong to various community service organizations and often took our children along to assist us. Outside of the feel-good factor that goes along with being part of something positive, volunteering gives you something impactful to do as a family and often brings you into contact with people in your local community who become good friends and/or strong business connections.

**The More You Give Away, the More That Comes Back**

Whether you call it the 'law of reciprocity,' karma, or just coincidence, giving can often have the boomerang effect of causing even more wealth to flow into your life. Giving can also benefit us in school and in our careers; volunteer hours are a part of the requirement for high school graduation and universities and employers often look at community involvement and extracurricular activities when considering you for a position.

Giving their time and resources tends to encourage generosity in kids as well as making them more aware of the world around them and more tolerant towards others. It broadens their perspective and their perception of how they can make a difference in the world. As our local community slowly and surely expands through technology to become a global community it becomes even more important for us to be involved in and aware of the wider world.

# Chapter 10

# Resolving Conflict

*"Children are in greater need
of models than critics"*
                    *Joseph Joubert*

Teaching kids to resolving conflicts helps to build confident and empowered children. Conflict is a normal part of children's lives. Having different needs or wants, or wanting the same thing, can easily lead children into conflict with one another. "She won't let me play the game!" "He took my video game controller!" "Alexa is being mean!" are grumbles that parents, teachers and counselors often hear when children get into conflict and are unable to resolve it. Children often respond to conflict by arguing with one another, using physical aggression, or by using more passive responses such as backing off and avoiding one another.

When conflict is poorly managed it can have a negative impact on children's relationships, on their self-esteem and on their overall learning. However, teaching children the skills for resolving conflict can help significantly. By learning to manage conflict effectively children's skills for getting along with others can be improved. Children are much happier, have better friendships and learn better at school when they know how to manage conflict well.

It's easy for parents to solve their children's conflicts. "Tyler, I saw you take David's action figure. Please give it back to your brother and then say you're sorry!" This type of parent interference does not empower children to solve their own conflicts or learn from these valuable opportunities. Conflict resolution is a learned skill; it takes repetitive practice. Parents can help their children develop this skill.

**Dealing with conflict in front of your children**

This is difficult. Life happens. When you are a parent, your children often see you in unflattering situations or are in earshot of your unbecoming conversations. It is a good idea to have moments when you discuss with your children how you made a mistake, how you said something "not so nice" about someone and how you made amends. Children need to see their parents go through the stages/motions of the friendship process/mistake. They watch everything that we say and do – so we might as well be honest so that they have a shot at becoming a decent human being. Children already think that their parents already have got it all together. We must take time to tell them of times that we made mistakes (even when we were their age) so that they can see that not everything is ready made. They need to see and experience the process of life.

**Steps and suggestions for conflict resolution with friends and siblings**

**1. Set the stage for WIN-WIN outcomes.** Conflict arises when people have different needs or views of a situation. Make it clear that you are going to help the children listen to each other's point of view and look for ways to solve the problem that everyone can agree to.

**Ask:** What's the problem here? Be sure to get both sides of the story. For example: "He won't let me have a turn" from one child, and "I only just started and it's my game," from another child. **Say:** I'm sure if we talk this through we'll be able to sort it out so that everyone has a fair opportunity to play the game.

**2. Have children state their own needs and concerns.** The goal is to find out how each child perceives the problem. Help your children identify and communicate their needs and concerns without judging or blaming.

**Ask:** What do you want or need? What are you most concerned about?

**3. Help children listen to the other person and understand their needs and concerns.** In the heat of conflict it is difficult to understand that the other person has feelings and needs too. Listening to the other person helps to reduce the conflict and allows children to think of the problem as something they can solve together.

**Ask:** So you want to have a turn at this game now because it's nearly time to go home? And you want to keep playing to see if you can get to the next level? Show children that you understand both points of view: I can understand why you want to get your turn. I can see why you don't want to stop now.

**4. Help children think of different ways to solve the problem.** Often children who get into conflict can only think of one solution. Getting them to think of creative ways for solving the conflict encourages them to come up with new solutions. Ask them to let the ideas flow and think of as many options as they can, without judging any of them.

**Encourage:** Let's think of at least three things we could do to solve this problem.

**5. Build win-win solutions.** Help children sort through the list of options you have come up with together and choose those that appear to meet each child's needs. Sometimes a combination of the options they have thought of will work best. Together, you can help them build a solution that everyone agrees to.

**Ask:** Which solution do you think can work? Which option can we make work together?

**6. Put the solution into action and see how it works.** Make sure that children understand what they have agreed to and what this means in practice.

**Say:** "Okay, so this is what we've agreed. Dillon, you're going to show Kyle how to play the game, then Kyle, you're going to have a try, and I'm going to let you know when 15 minutes is up (or you can set a timer so that the children can be even be more independent when working with their conflict)."

### Teach Them Forgiveness

Forgiveness shows your child that mistakes are a natural part of learning. It is a hard virtue to teach. It requires that we lay down our right to be angry over an offense committed against us—a tough sell in this crazy world where we're encouraged to "look out for number one."

But there's one sense in which choosing forgiveness is looking out for number one: it gives you a chance to be happy, and to release the burden of those hard feelings you're carrying around. Forgive your child for any wrong-doing once the situation has been dealt with. As a parent, you should want your children to be forgiving people! Those who know how to forgive and move on are happier people with better relationships.

Here are some ways that parents can model this important life lesson for their children in everyday circumstances.

**1. Show forgiveness to your children.** Sometimes our kids' behavior doesn't just break a rule, it breaks our hearts (or makes us mad as heck). Of course, we have the responsibility in all circumstances to address and correct the behavior, and to enact disciplinary measures when needed. But your child knows the difference between discipline given in anger and discipline given to help them. If you are still angry or hurt because of something that your child did, take a time out before you engage with your child about their consequences. If they are aware of your anger or frustration, proactively offer your forgiveness before you proceed with correction. Even if they don't seem to understand that they need your forgiveness, offer it anyway. One day they will understand.

**2. Try to model forgiveness in your marriage/partnership/relationship.** Your children have a front-row seat to the lengthy play that is your marriage. They see the miscommunication, the juice that dad agreed to pick up and forgot, the laundry you promised to make time to fold and never got around to. Your children are watching to see how each of you reacts when the other makes a mistake. In every one of these instances—and certainly in the bigger marriage crises—you have a choice. Each time you choose to forgive your spouse and work together to move forward, you're teaching your children a priceless lesson.

**3. Practice forgiveness in your other community and school relationships.** That teacher or coach who dropped the ball and upset your child? Forgive them. Especially if it was an isolated incident. (Ex: "I know Coach Samson embarrassed you today, but that's not like her. Maybe she was just having a bad day. Let's forgive her and move on. If it happens again, we can talk to her about it.") The church staff member or committee member who hurt your feelings or ruffle your feathers? Same thing. Your kids hear you talk about these things and are more aware of the small dramas in your life than you probably know. Handle them in a way that you'd want them to emulate.

**4. Show forgiveness in extended family relationships.** Some of the longest-standing grudges in world are held by members in your family. If your parents were divorced and your childhood was rocky, you may still be dragging around the baggage. Your prior failed marriage may have left you with hurts that you've never laid down. For your own sake, and for the benefit of your kids, call it quits on being angry and let it go. You'll be glad you did.

## General principles for helping your children resolve conflict:

1) The ways that parents and adults respond to children's conflicts have powerful effects on children's behavior and skill development.

2) Until they have developed their own skills for managing conflict effectively most children will need very specific adult guidance to help them reach a good resolution.

3) Parents, educators and counselors can help children to see conflict as a shared problem that can be solved by understanding both points of view and finding a solution that everyone is happy with.

## Facilitate and coach

When parents impose a solution on children it may solve the conflict in the short term, but it can leave children feeling that their wishes have not been taken into account. Coaching children through the conflict resolution steps helps them feel involved. It shows them how effective conflict resolution can work so that they can start to build their own skills.

## Listen to all sides without judging

To learn the skills for effective conflict resolution, children need to be able to acknowledge their own point of view and listen to others' views without fearing that they will be blamed or judged. Being heard encourages children to hear and understand what others have to say and how they feel. Support children to work through difficult feelings. Conflict often generates difficult feelings such as anger or anxiety. Difficult feelings get in the way of being able to think through conflicts fairly and reasonably. Acknowledge children's difficult feelings and help them to manage them. It may be necessary to help children calm down before trying to resolve the conflict.

Please remember to praise children for finding a solution and carrying it out in a peaceful manner. If an agreed solution doesn't work out the first time, go through the steps again to find a different solution that may work.

# Chapter 11

# Health & Wellness

Although we often describe children as "tiny adults," physically, a child's body is different from that of an adult, and because healthy children are continuously growing and developing, they have specific dietary requirements and needs. Giving children nutritionally condensed food options is vital for their appropriate growth and development. A child's body needs nutrition, not just food. According to kidshealth.org, one out of three children in America is overweight or obese. Allowing children to eat processed and fast foods instead of providing a balance of fruits, vegetables and other complete foods can lead to weight issues. Healthy eating is needed for healthy development. If nutritional requirements are unmet because too many sugary and high-fat foods are replacing nourishing food, children may be unable to perform at age-appropriate levels. Children have a higher metabolic rate, requiring more caloric consumption than adults, but it's vital that the calories they consume be nutritious.

Diet and nutrition are key factors in the health and growth of your children. All children require lots of nutrients to help their bodies develop all the necessary functions and tissues they need, and the quality (or lack thereof) of these nutrients can have a big impact on their overall health. Everything from basic brain function to behavioral patterns can be influenced by the diet a child eats. Nutrition is also involved in the prevention of many childhood diseases, especially conditions like obesity and diabetes.

**Encourage good eating habits**

When it comes to healthy eating and food preferences, it has been my experience that children can fall anywhere on a wide-ranging spectrum. My children were on different spectrums of eating. My daughter was an extremely picky eater while my son has always been the adventurous gourmand who is ready, willing, and able to try new foods and dishes. But no matter what kind of healthy eating habits your children have developed, you can help shape his/her preferences and attitudes toward nutritious food by guiding them toward healthy eating habits. Here's how I worked my magic with food:

**Go grocery/food shopping with your kids to teach**

**healthy eating choices**. One way that I showed my children healthy eating choices was to fill up my grocery cart with fresh produce and discuss how I was planning to cut down on processed foods. I tried to make a game out of picking out different colors of fruits and vegetables. Both my son and daughter got in on the action and really became competitive with this game. We tried to think about meals that we could make for the coming week, such as a stir-fry (green broccoli, yellow and red peppers, orange carrots, and so on).

**Let Your Kids Help You Cook.** Whatever age your children are, encourage them to help in the kitchen. When my daughter was in first grade, she was not quite able to chop vegetables, but she could tear up lettuce for the salad, place the rolls in a basket and set the table. My son was two years older and was able to stir sauces and measure out the ingredients that I had written out on the white board. I was always glad that I encouraged culinary habits early when my children were younger. Once they got older it was easier for them to feel confident about whipping up a delicious dinner for the whole family.

**Don't Stress About the Amount of Food Your Young Children Eat.** When my son was growing up, he seemed to polish off everything on his plate one day and then eat two peas and declare that he was done the next. This is perfectly normal behavior for a growing child. It is our job as parents not to make kids feel bad for not finishing everything on their plate. I would often try to head off problems at the pass by offering smaller portions (and letting the kids know that there were always seconds if they finished and were truly hungry).

**Encourage Smart Snacking.** Even if your child is served a favorite dish for dinner, he/she may not eat it if they snacked too close to mealtime and aren't hungry. Try not to let them snack at least an hour before dinner, and if they do have something, try to make it as healthy and light as possible—say, baby carrots with hummus or apple slices.

**Avoid the Allure of Bribes.** Trust me…this is a hard one. It is SO tempting to say no TV, dessert, or whatever else your children want unless he/she eats their dinner. But this can create an uneasy relationship with food in your children. Instead of making them feel pressured into eating when they don't feel like it, give them choices that are more likely to go down easy, such as bite-sized portions of cheesy broccoli or a fruit smoothie—healthy choices they will want to eat.

**Begin Your Child's Day With A Nourishing Breakfast.** It's the most important meal of the day, but one in four children in Australia skips breakfast. At school, a hungry child can lose concentration in class, have no energy for playtime and snack on unhealthy foods, such as chips or biscuits. A calm and healthy breakfast every day is the best defense against this happening. It also helps children to get into good habits that they can carry through life.

**Breakfast Ideas:** Breakfast can include all sorts of options: cereals, bread, fruit, dairy products (such as eggs, milk, yogurt, breakfast protein (sausage, bacon or veggie meat and any types of cheese. Several factors influence what people like to eat at breakfast, such as their food preferences, cultural background, religious beliefs and the time available before they must head out the door.

**Quick and easy breakfast ideas:**

- Cereal with milk, yogurt and/or fruit
- Whole grain toast, raisin bread or muffins with fruit spreads, Nutella or slices of banana
- Fresh fruit with yogurt
- Fruit smoothies made with fresh or canned fruit
- Toaster waffles/pancakes with warm milk and a piece of fruit
- Omelet with lean meat and tomatoes
- Boiled egg with bread fingers (cut slices of bread into dipping sized portions)
- Pancakes with fresh fruit filling or fruit on top
- Whole Grain toast or fresh bread with eggs (not fried), cooked mushrooms or tomatoes
- Plain whole grain muffin with lean bacon and cooked tomatoes

It is also important to have healthy drinks with breakfast. Water or low-fat milk (for children over two years) is best.

Try to limit fruit juice to 1/2 a glass a day as fruit juice contains lots of sugar. Instead give a piece of fruit to your child to get fiber into their diet.

Handy tip: Discourage your child from eating breakfast in front of the television. This can also help speed up your morning routines!

**Don't Ban Junk Food**

Ha! One of my favorites...junk food! This doesn't mean allowing your young children to eat a Little Debbie Snack Cake a day (like my daughter did for about two straight weeks once!) Limiting processed food that's high in sugar and calories is a good idea. But if you try to forbid so much as a lollipop in your home, your child is more likely to scarf up all the sugar he can find at a friend's house. A better way to handle sugary snacks is to let kids have a piece of candy or chocolate every once in a while, and if they clamor for something sweet, try to steer them toward healthy snacks such as nuts with raisins the rest of the time.

**Set a Good Example**

If you ban soda from your children's diets and then they see you guzzle down a Sprite over dinner, it sends them a mixed message. Take some time and examine your own attitude toward food (do you try healthy recipes or eat fatty foods and then express remorse and worry about your own weight aloud?). If you are willing to find new ways to get creative with healthy choices, your young children will be more likely to follow in your footsteps.

# Chapter 12

# The Tough Topics

There are many challenging subjects we should talk to our children about, first. Many parents like to shy away from the tough topics but the scary truth is if they don't learn about these important subjects from you, they will learn about them from their peers-and we don't want that. The difficult conversations are imperative because they can give you the opportunity to guide your child towards sensible and responsible decisions and to talk through your family values. Don't be afraid to talk to your child about drugs, relationships, breaking the law, depression, suicide, drinking, physical violence, bullying, peer pressure, safety…well, you get the point. Your child needs your guidance and should not be left with the responsibility of figuring these out on their own.

I will admit these subjects can become awkward

conversations that often produce eye-rolling and moans from our preteens and teenagers. But not dealing with them can be a life or death situation. If you are feeling overwhelmed just thinking about how to bring all of these tricky conversations without getting the typical exasperated response from your child? Experts say that children are more easily drawn into an in-depth discussion when their parents ask questions about their opinions instead of being lectured. I recommend that you start your discussions with some open-ended questions, such as:

**Dating**
- What does dating mean to you?
- Does anyone you know date?
- What do they do?
- Where do they go?
- Pick a couple you know of who you think has a decent relationship and a couple who you think has an unhealthy relationship.
- Why did you choose these couples?

**Abusive Relationships**
- Do you think there is a right way to argue?
- Do you think there are unfair ways to argue?
- Have you ever seen any kind of abusive behavior between two people who were dating?
- Why do you think someone would abuse their boyfriend or girlfriend?
- What do you think makes a healthy relationship?

**Sex**
- Are there a lot of kids that talk about sex?
- Do you have any questions about what sex is or what the consequences of sex too early are?

**Friends and Peer Pressure**
- Who are some of your best friends?
- What are some of the things that you like about your friends?
- What are some things you don't like about how your friends act or how they treat you?
- Why do you think we are so vulnerable to the influence of our friends and peers?
- Have you seen anyone stand up to peer pressure? What happened?

**Bullying**
- What does it mean to stand up for yourself? When you stand up for yourself, how does it make you feel?
- Do you know anyone who has been bullied? How did they handle it?
- Do you think most of the kids in your school are mean or nice to each other?
- Can you think of ways to avoid or stop bullying?
- Do you think online bullying is getting worse or better?
- Have you ever felt like a bystander? What happened? How did you handle it?

**Social Media**
- What kind of social media do most of your friends use the most?
- What do you like about it?
- Do you think social media is helpful or harmful?
- How do you like to use social media?
- How do you feel when you use social media – happy, sad, anxious?
- Do you know anyone who has sexted? Did they get in trouble?

**Drugs / Alcohol**
- Do you know people who buy (or sell) drugs and/or prescriptions?
- Are there a lot of kids that talk about alcohol?
- Have you ever seen people drink or get high at school or at a friend's house or at a party?
- Do you know people who drive after drinking or using drugs?
- Do you know anyone who has posted a drunk picture or video of themselves – or someone else – on social media? What happened when people saw it?
- Has anyone you know ever gotten sick after drinking or doing drugs?

These are just some examples of how to ask "curious" (not accusatory) questions of your teen to get their input and opinions and begin a healthy conversation. As you address these tricky subjects with your child, here are a few additional tips to remember:

1) Take time to educate yourself. Please do not attempt to have a conversation with your child about an important topic if you have no idea what you're talking about. Take some time to breathe, clear your mind of any bias, research the subject and talk to other parents before you begin the conversation with your child.

2) Revisit the subject at a different time/day. It is not a great idea to have "the talk," in which you try to tell your children everything they need to know in one single conversation. Experts always recommend that you have ongoing conversations, addressing issues as your child matures.

3) Try to stay calm. No matter what your child says, check your bias and do not get angry or judgmental. Continue asking questions to gather information. If you feel overwhelmed and not sure how to handle the conversation or you are not sure what to say, simply let your child know that they have brought up some interesting points and you'd like to talk about it again after you've had some time to think. Do not pretend to know everything.

4) Be prepared and have resources in case your child asks more questions. One of the best things you can do for your child is to guide them to trustworthy resources to get more information on a topic. Sometimes your word as a parent is the seed – but other reputable resources will allow the child to process thoughts and provide more information. Perhaps purchase books on the subject, introduce them to experts in certain fields, cut out a newspaper article, or encourage your child to ask their doctor questions by giving them an opportunity to meet alone when they have an appointment.

**How to deal with peer pressure and bullying**

I was working with a teenager that once seriously considered taking her own life. Having been the brunt of extreme bullying and peer pressure since she schools, Ashley's mental health started to decline. The now 20-year-old's breaking point came when she was in her first year of college. Ashley, who was highly involved in school events as a three-sport athlete, was a target of social media bullying. Over time, the bullying became more personal in nature and some began to physically threaten her life. Scared for her life and unaware of who to turn to for help, Ashley filed a restraining order against her online attacker who also happened to be a former friend.

"I felt peer pressure when I spoke up about my story and my mental health," says Ashley. "I was told things like maybe I asked for it and that the best thing to do was walk away. So, I felt this pressure from my environment to not speak out. I would get comments (even from adults in my life) that if I was to speak out about how sad or depressed that I had become because of the situation, that I would appear different and unstable and that no one would want to become my friend."

As a result of the mounting pressures, Ashley gave in to their bad advice and stayed silent. She eventually retreated into herself and was forced to take time off from school. What made the situation worse was that her parents and family members had no clue what was going on. "At first I wanted to make it seem like everything was OK, but deep inside I was crumbling," she says. "It came to a point where I knew I really needed help and needed to talk to my family about this when I contemplated taking my own life." Ashley eventually pursued help from a psychologist and now uses her experience to educate others as a youth mental health advocate with organizations that are a part of her university.

While her story has a relatively happy ending, many other students who attempt to combat bullying or peer pressure can't say the same. In fact, according to most institutes of health research, at least one in three children have reported feeling peer pressured and bullied. Parents continue to talk to your children and encourage your children to open up about this.

**The different types of peer pressure**

When people hear the words "peer pressure," they tend to think of negatives. But, Fairholm says, that isn't always the case."What parents need to understand is that (peer pressure) is one of the developmental tasks for youth," says Fairholm. "At this time in their lives they're trying to learn how to negotiate their social relationships and how to be with friends and other groups. So this is what they go through as they work their way toward being an adult and it really is about belonging." That means kids will have to face both negative and positive peer pressures as they age.

According to a study published in 2014 by the National Center for Biotechnology Information (NCBI), teens tend to alter the way they think about taking risks when they're with other teens and are more likely to engage in risky behavior if their friends positively reinforce their actions. In fact, research out of the University of Melbourne in 2011 revealed that young men tend to be influenced most by other young men they consider friends; for young women, the pressures come from boyfriends or strangers.

But, as noted above, peer pressure can also be used as a positive tool for kids to put their energy into influencing their peers to get involved with issues, healthy activities and so on. According to a 2013 Penn State study, children will exhibit fewer behaviour problems if they feel their peers are willing to encourage them to behave well.

**Peer pressure vs. bullying**

When kids use their power over kids they perceive to be less powerful to cause harm, it is classified as bullying, says Fairholm. The Respect Education Program spoke to Global News to offer her tips. "It becomes a negative act on the kids being targeted," Fairholm says. "But it also becomes a negative act for the kids who are acting this way because they are learning false messages about power, who they are and how they belong."

There's a fine line between bullying and peer pressure, however. Often, if a person doesn't want to take part in an activity their friends will drop the taunting, according to the Kids Helpline. But when the taunting persists and the person feels threatened, forced or isolated from their group, then that's when the peer pressure is considered to be bullying. And if that line is crossed and the bullying is persistent, kids may experience depression or anxiety worse than compared to if they were the victim of abuse, says a University of Warwick study.

**Signs your child could be a target of negative pressures**

Initial signs to pay attention to are if the child is being secretive, withdrawing from relationships or activities and showing disrespect toward others, says Fairholm."If you see there is a big change in your child's behavior, it's important to know that all behaviour has meaning," says Fairholm. "But remember there is a normal level of that with the adolescent years because their bodies are changing, their hormones are all over the place and sometimes they don't know what's happening inside of them."

**What parents need to know about 'ghost apps' used to hide sexts**

Fairholm says if the changes in children's behaviour are extreme and out of character, parents should begin to dig deeper to find the cause. If the child is focusing on their image, making comparisons to others and struggling in school, these may be signs as well says uKnowKids.com. Other signs to look for include sleeping troubles, loss of appetite or overeating and low moods.

According to RaisingChildren.net, children with poor self-esteem who feel they have few friends and those who have special needs are more likely to be negatively influenced by peers.

**What can you do as a parent?**

Talk to your kids about healthy relationships. "Talk about the importance of respecting other people and boundaries and what it means to have relationships and include people," Fairholm says. "And look at what you're modelling in the home when it comes to communication and how the family deals with conflict and respecting boundaries and set a good example." If parents suspect their child is the target of negative peer pressure, it's better to deal with the situation as early as possible, she adds. "I think it's really hard as a parent when you start to think that something isn't adding up," Fairholm says. "Parents need to recognize the signs. Rather than getting mad or thinking it will go away, they need to deal with it and find out what's happening in their child's life."

Parents also need to have ongoing open discussions with their child without getting angry. "Parents need to deal with these issues calmly," she says. "They need to start setting structure and expectations around the child and hold the child to that structure and expectations." It's also important to remember that if kids need someone to talk to and aren't comfortable speaking with their parents, they can turn to another family member, a counselor or a service like the Kids Help Phone for advice.

# Chapter 13

# Affirm Your Child

Praising a child is a wonderful way to raise their self-confidence and reinforce good behavior and actions that you would like to see more of from them. Just like adults children need to hear positive words of encouragement and affirmation. Positive reinforcement and praise is always better than criticism and punishment. At every point and juncture in your children's life, affirm them. Concentrate on what you like about your child and comment on it. Congratulate your child for doing well. Continuously remind them that they are unique, valued, loved. Too many children grow up in homes where they're marginalized, being either told or implied that they are hopeless, worthless and won't amount to anything. Affirmation sets a peaceful tone in the home because it is person-affirming. Affirmations are a widespread strategy used for positively programming your child's subconscious mind and can be used as a motivational tool to enhance their self-esteem. Affirmations are clear, concise, positive suggestions designed to influence their subconscious to create a specific outcome. There are so many voices in this world telling our kids they don't measure up.

**Behind every young child should be a parent who believes in him/her, is a parent who believed in him/her first.**

**Make it about them.** What we ultimately want is for our children to develop their own power of self-evaluation, rather than become "praise junkies," dependent on us to tell them if they are doing well. Instead of "I'm so proud of you," you can help them realize their own achievements saying instead, "You have worked hard and did really well on this test. Do you feel proud of yourself?" and once they answer "Yes," you can always add, "I am proud of you too!"

**Be selective in your praise.** Praise everything your child does and he or she will either discount what you are saying, or they will become dependent on praise from others for self-affirmation. Do not overdo it.

**Praise the effort.** When we focus on our children's effort, rather than their achievement. we encourage them to learn the art of motivation and self-evaluation: "Yes I worked really hard to get to this result so it's worth making the effort in the future."

**Praise descriptively rather than using "evaluative" praise.** Instead of saying "Wow, this is so beautiful," ask your child a question. For example: "How did you do this part?" or "How did you make the dog in your drawing look so lifelike?" Your child will appreciate that you have taken an interest in his or her work and how it was executed and is more likely to realize his or her achievements and start talking about their work.

**Praise specific actions rather than their overall behavior.** This allows your child to realize that a behavior is something that they *choose* rather than something they *are*. For example, instead of saying "You were really good when Grandma was here," you can say "I really appreciated that you helped Grandma with her coat during her visit today."

**Accentuate the positive, reduce the negative.** Make sure that your positives outweigh the negatives so that you fill your child's "I can do it" account instead of filling the "I can't do it" account. For example, rather than saying, "No, that's not the way to do this," suggest, "I see that you've done it this way. There is another way that you could have also done it. Can I show you another way?"

**Try not to criticize.** Even constructive criticism can be interpreted by your child as being negative. You need to try and always identify the good things in something that you child has done and ask the child to explain the reason for his success (usually the effort that they've put into it). This helps fill the "I'm capable" account. If you feel that there is room for improvement, you can then add, "What could you better next time?"

**Be honest.** Even young children see through false praise. It is important to remain honest. If you're not impressed by your child's achievement, you don't have to label their actions as good or bad and can just mention something like: "I see that you're practicing your ...." And this lets your child know she has your attention.

**Let your child eavesdrop.** Make sure your child overhears you praising something that he or she did to your partner or friend (but don't overdo it, boastful parents are rarely popular).

**You don't always need to say something.** Sometimes giving them a smile or a hug can be more powerful that using words. So, if your child is struggling with their self-esteem, try arming them with some of the affirmations below. But before you get started, there are four rules that parents should follow when creating affirmations.

**1) Any affirmations you say to your child should be short, positive and stated in the present tense.**
Remember the subliminal is the bottom line; if the

affirmations are too long, wordy, or negatively stated, it may create some confusion and forfeit their outcome – so cut to the chase.

**2) Be sure your child repeats the affirmations silently with their eyes closed and with strong, sincere emotion.** Their attitude and social-emotional intensity will subconsciously place their affirmations with priority status.

**3) The ideal time for your child to REPEAT their affirmations to them again as they are drifting off to sleep.** Their final thoughts while entering sleep will be filed away at a deep subconscious level creating stronger lasting impressions and quicker results.

**4) Avoid affirmations containing the word "don't."** A child's mind will always overlook a double-negative. If you tell a child, "Don't slam the door," the brain does not register the word "don't" and instead hears the command, "slam the door." As a result, they will slam that door hard. The word "don't" is too abstract for their mind to comprehend. You will get a better result if you say, "Close the door quietly." In this case they hear the word, "quietly" instead of the word, "slam."

Here are some solid self-esteem affirmations to help your children get started. My husband and I have successfully used all of these with our own children, so I hope these have the same success with your children:

# **100 Affirmations**

1) *I think you're fantastic!*
2) *You did a great Job!*
3) *Thank you for being such a great kid!*
4) *Your uniqueness makes me smile.*
5) *I appreciate the young man (woman) you are becoming.*
6) *I really like you.*
7) *Spending time with you reminds me of how special you are.*
8) *Would you like to go to the store with me? I like it when you come along.*
9) *You are such an interesting person.*
10) *I really like how your mind works.*
11) *Thank you for being such a hard worker.*
12) *You are such a good example for your younger siblings / or for your friends.*
13) *I was just telling your Mom/Dad how proud I am of you.*
14) *I'm very grateful God gave you to me.*
15) *You did that so well.*
16) *Terrific job on your homework!*
17) *You're so handsome/beautiful.*
18) *You have such a clear way of seeing things.*
19) *Good thinking.*
20) *You give the best hugs.*
21) *You are so brave!*
22) *That was a really kind thing to do.*
23) *You're so smart!*

24) Thank you for honoring me.
25) You are a great person.
26) You are the kind of friend I wish I had when I was your age.
27) Wow! You're so fast!
28) You are a really thoughtful person.
29) I appreciate you so much.
30) You are a diligent young man/woman.
31) You make me so happy!
32) You have such a great sense of humor.
33) Wow! Did you do that? You are amazing!
34) You are an honest young man/woman – I love that.
35) Wow! You did a great job cleaning your room!
36) You made this all by yourself? It tastes fantastic!
37) What a terrific idea!
38) You have got a lot of 'grit'!
39) I'm so happy when you're around.
40) Look at all those muscles! (when your child is very young)
41) I am really very proud of you.
42) You have such a big heart!
43) You are so generous.
44) You inspire people when you do things like that!
45) When you did (... ) it showed a lot of self-discipline.
46) How did I get so lucky to have the Best Kid in The World?
47) I just know that you are going to be successful.
48) You have some remarkable gifts.
49) You can accomplish anything you desire.

*50) God created you for a special purpose.*

*51) Your life matters.*

*52) I don't know where you're going to end up, but I know that it is going to be awesome!*

*53) You are such a tough cookie!*

*54) I love how you never give up!*

*55) You could run a small country! Maybe a large one!!*

*56) You have such a strong sense of character.*

*57) You are one in a million!*

*58) I value your opinion. What do you think about this?*

*59) I don't deserve a daughter/son like you!*

*60) You make being proud of your son/daughter so easy.*

*61) You could be President someday!*

*62) Keep practicing like that and you're going to be the best in the world!*

*63) You showed a lot of courage when you ( )*

*64) It takes a big person to be honest like you just were.*

*65) I know that you can conquer your fears!*

*66) You have got what it takes!*

*67) You are a real go-getter!*

*68) Do you know how unique people like you are?*

*69) You are a really polite person – I like that in a young man/young woman.*

*70) You do some quality work!*

*71) I am very grateful for you.*

*72) You are a blessing to me and Mom/Dad.*

*73) There is no one quite like you.*

*74) How did you come up with that?*

75) *It is a rare thing to find someone trustworthy like you.*
76) *I know that you can figure it out!*
77) *You worked until the job was complete – that is impressive!*
78) *When you stood up for what was right, that made me SO very proud of you!"*
79) *You are looking so good today!*
80) *You are a special individual.*
81) *God wanted to bless me, so He gave me you.*
82) *What a great job you did!*
83) *I know that you will achieve your dreams.*
84) *This world would be a better place if more people were like you.*
85) *You figured this out by yourself? Amazing!*
86) *What you did for your (me, friend, brother, sister) was really kind.*
87) *Grandpa and/or Grandma think that you are a spectacular person!*
88) *You are really going places!*
89) *You showed a lot of maturity when you responded like that.*
90) *I can see your future . . . it is so bright, I'm going to need some good sunglasses!*
91) *You are the son/daughter I prayed for.*
92) *Every parent wishes they had a son/daughter like you.*
93) *I don't know what I would do without you.*
94) *I love the fact that I (our family) can rely on you.*
95) *Dad/Mom and I were just talking about how wonderful you are.*

*96) Thank you for loving me.*
*97) I can see your inner strength.*
*98) You stood for the Truth – that's what good people do!*
*99) Awesome – that's what you are!*
*100) I love you!*

# Index 1

## The ABCs of *Socially Wize* Parents

**Socially Wize parents:**

**A – Appreciate** the ever-changing nature of parenting so that when their child progresses to a new developmental stage, or the family opens a new chapter in their family history, they will behave appropriately as the parent.

**B – Balance** their life commitments (i.e. work, hobbies, friends) with their family commitments so that they are truly present for both their family and their non-family activities.

**C – Consistently** provide instruction, discipline, praise, or appreciation for their child as the situation warrants – they do not avoid doing these things because they are tired, overwhelmed with other life commitments, or are finding it difficult to see the point in the moment.

**D – Dig Deeper** within themselves when the act of parenting during a difficult moment seems too difficult, thankless, or overwhelming. They might not realize it during an emotional situation with their child, but the long-term benefits of consistent, strategic parenting are invaluable to every child.

**E – Encourage** their child to be themselves. Our kids do not need to be a younger imitation of ourselves to be successful people. It does not make you a bad parent if your child is not exactly like you! Socially Wize Parents guide their child into being who they were meant to be.

**F – Forgive** their child for their wrong-doing once the situation has been dealt with it between parent and child.

**G – Generously** give their child their time, patience, and (most importantly!) their love.

**H – Have** a support system in place. Socially Wize Parents surround themselves with friends and extended family members who are supportive of their parenting.

**I – Include** personal time for yourself that will enable you to grow, recharge, and to become a better person. Taking some personal time for yourself has two important benefits: 1) it models for your child how an adult balances life responsibilities with personal pleasure and 2) this time allows you as a parent to blow off some parenting steam and return to your family with a clear head and sound heart.

**J – Just** follow the parenting plan. It is hard to parent a child effectively during an emotional situation – that is why Socially Wize Parents make a plan before their child misbehaves. This insures that they will parent appropriately during a high-stress situation.

**K – Keep** it simple. Parenting does not have to be complicated to work.

**L – Limit-set.** This is a key principle in Socially Wize Parenting and one that needs to be updated every time a child enters into a new developmental phase. Socially Wize Parents learn to adapt their limit-setting standards as their child shows that they can handle more responsibility on their own.

**M – Model** the behavior that they want from their child in their own day-to-day actions. Children learn best by observing what their parents *DO* rather than by what their parents *SAY*.

**N – Nourish** their child's heart. Socially Wize Parents listen when their child needs to talk. They hug their child when they need support. They are physically and mentally present when their child needs them. They show up when it matters.

**O – Organize** their non-family commitments (i.e. work,

hobbies, friendships, etc.) in a way that prioritizes their family.

**P – Passions,** values, and beliefs – this is the Socially Wize Parent's "code of conduct" and these standards provide a guide for all Socially Wize Parenting decisions. Do you need help creating your own family passions, values, and beliefs?

**Q – Quick** action – Socially Wize Parents don't let a situation with their child drag on without addressing it with their child. If your child misbehaves, then handle it right away. Don't know how to handle the situation? Follow your pre-designed parenting plan (that takes into account your family passions, vales, and beliefs) as a guide.

**R – Reexamine** their parenting skills on an annual basis – what is working for them and their family and what is not? Where can they improve?

**S – Strategize** their discipline and include that in their parenting plan so that they know how they are going to handle specific problem situations with their child.

**T – Take** time out for personal reflection and setting goals for the family on a regular basis. Because family dynamics are constantly changing, Socially Wize Parents will need to update their family goals on a yearly basis.

**U – Understand** that Socially Wize Parenting takes time, is hard work, and is often inconvenient (i.e. kids get sick right before an important meeting or they want to have a heart-to heart talk with you when you are exhausted after a hard day) and that it the most honorable and rewarding obligation Socially Wize Parents will ever be called to do in their life.

**V – Value** the relationship they have with their child.

**W – Wisdom** – Socially Wize Parenting requires wise decision-making using a parenting plan over rash, grandiose actions lecturing the child in front of other people just to "look like a good parent."

**X – eXpect** changes to occur in the family often. Kids grow into new developmental stages (just as you have mastered the parenting skills needed during the previous one!), and family situations can change due to employment changes, new siblings entering the family, etc. Socially Wize Parents don't expect life to remain exactly the same; therefore, they are better able to handle the changes when they appear.

**Y – Yield** to new parenting habits that might seem unnatural at first. Many parents that I work with give up on using new (more beneficial) parenting skills because when they used these skills the first time, they felt weird doing them. New habits take practice and it is in practicing new skills and habits MANY TIMES OVER do we start to feel comfortable. Socially Wize Parents don't give up!

**Z – Zero** in on what's important. Socially Wize Parents understand that drama happens inside and outside of the family dynamics, but it is not as important as what is going on with their child and/or your spouse/partner. Always take care of yourself, your child, and your spouse/partner first before attempting to get involved with other people's problems.

# *Index*

## Family fun for all ages

Creating fun activities with your younger children can be part of your family's everyday life. Many of the ideas in this chapter might be routines you are doing already. If there are some new ideas, we hope you will use them. The more you enjoy spending time with your children, the more they will be able to learn. Your children's abilities to learn many skills in the early years will depend on their stages of development and their individual interests. In addition, their learning will depend on the opportunities and support that the family offers them at home and in their surroundings. Here are a few helpful hints to assist you in planning and doing the activities with your children.

☒ Establish some rules with your children and be consistent

about enforcing them. Set limits and be prepared to have them tested!
- Use eye contact and reasoning to relate positively to your children.
- Give detailed explanations to questions and explain the meanings of new words when you're playing with young children.
- Assigning a few simple household chores helps your children learn to follow directions.
- Outdoor activities will give your children a chance to use some energy and stay healthy!
- It is also important to praise your children for their positive behaviors and let them know they are loved.

Children are constantly learning, especially when they are playing. Learning for children should be fun. Learning and playing with your children should also be fun for parents. You will find that your child is curious and eager to talk and play with you.

## SociallyWize Fun Activities for Parents and Younger Children

### In the Kitchen

In the kitchen, you and your children can do many things together: put away groceries, prepare meals and snacks, set the table. Every family member can have a job to do! Your children will feel good about their successes as they use their large and small muscles and look for shapes and colors. Be sure the kitchen is a safe place. Keep sharp objects out of reach. Remind your children about family rules in the kitchen.

Help your children become aware of differences in foods.

- Talk with your children about the size, taste, texture, and color of foods. Help them to recognize the differences between rough and smooth surfaces, salty or sweet tastes, and the odors of certain foods.
- Ask them to talk about changes in foods as you cook them ("How did it look when it was raw?... when we started to cook it?... how does it look now?"). Help your children to compare the before and after.
- Talk with your children about any foods that have special meaning to your family.

Look for shapes or colors around the kitchen in and on the cabinets, refrigerator and stove.

- Ask your children to find circles, triangles, or squares.
- Play the game, *"I see something you don't see and the color (or the shape) IS..."* Your children can name the items or foods that are in the kitchen and that fit the description until they get to the item you have in mind.

Set the table with your children.

- Ask your children to make sure there is one plate, one glass, and so on, for each person.
- Talk about how to handle the dishes and silverware, so they stay clean and unbroken.

Involve your children in meal preparation.

- All family members preparing food need to wash their hands before handling food.
- Measure with cups, tablespoons, and teaspoons. Ask your children to guess how many tablespoons make a cup of water. Then, help them check it out!
- Let your children pour water with spoons, cups, and pitchers.
- Involve your children in making part of a meal or a snack.
- Talk about opposites big and small, hard and soft.

Sort and name foods after a trip to the grocery store.

- Let your children name each food or ask them to tell you something about each food, as you take it out of the bag.
- As you sort the groceries, ask your children to put together all the foods that are the same: fresh vegetables in one place, boxes in another place.
- Talk with your children about the sizes of cans as you put them away—tall and short, wide and narrow.

Name kitchen appliances and their uses.

- ☒ Ask your children what the toaster is for, what the oven does. Give safety tips for the use of each appliance and talk about who can turn them on and off.
- ☒ Ask about other ways to toast bread, heat the leftovers. The answers might be very creative!

Let your children help clean up the kitchen.

- ☒ Ask them to sort eating and cooking utensils by type or use.
- ☒ Let them wipe the table after meals. Encourage them to wipe the table from left to right and collect all the crumbs in one corner.

**In the Living Room/Family Room**

The Living Room or Family Room can be the place for both quiet and noisy activities. Your children will develop their social skills by learning how to be by themselves or how to be a part of the family group. Tell your child which items in the room are on the "Do Not Touch" list. These are activities to build both large and small muscles. The family room is a busy place!

Talk about sounds.

- ☒ Ask your children to point to the direction of the sound

and describe it.
- Ask you children to tell you about all the things that make loud or soft sounds such as the TV, the radio.
- Sing songs together: old favorites, nursery rhymes. Use a wooden spoon or thick stick as microphone.

Talk about:

- The names of all the furniture in the room, such as the lamp, table, and couch.
- Family stories about the children's grandparents, family histories and when your children were babies.
- The things your children make.
- Your children's favorite TV shows.

Develop your children's big muscles.

- Encourage your children to help with household jobs: watering plants, sweeping, dusting, vacuuming.
- You and the children can imitate characters from a story or a TV show.
- Act out what these people do. Help your children to find things around the house for dress-up or to add to the make-believe!
- Turn on music and march around the house. Or, if your family likes to dance, turn on music and have fun!

Read to your children each day.

- Give your children a chance to imitate reading to you from magazines, books, and newspapers. Have a special place for books and magazines.
- Make a "booklet" with your children by helping them cut out magazine pictures and paste them on paper--a "house book" or "animal book." Use other suggestions from your children.
- Ask an older child or other family member to read to a younger child and to you.

Talk about what it means to be a family member.

- Ask your children to name the members of your family and draw pictures.
- Discuss how members of the family help each other.
- Invite some older family members to tell stories.
- You may wish to write a story about your family or write down stories your children tell you about the family.

Let your children know that they are an important part of the family.

- Give your children a place to store their special treasures.
- Find a place to display your children's "work," such as hanging their artwork on the wall or a door.

**In one of the bedrooms**

The bedroom can be a special place to play alone or to share conversations and spend time with your child. You and your children can read stories and talk about almost anything! Your children will learn a lot of self-help skills in the bedroom. They will be very proud of their new abilities.

Read to your children daily.

- Tell a story or read a book to your children at bedtime.
- After you've finished reading, ask your children to tell you all they remember about the story.
- Encourage your children to make up and tell stories or repeat a story you have read.

Let your children know that books are special.

- Make a library shelf or book area with your children.
- Use different print materials often: borrowing from the library, making homemade books, and looking at junk mail, greeting cards, newspapers, or magazines.

Talk about clothing.

- Help your children describe pieces of clothing.
- Talk about the front and back, top and bottom of shirts, pants, skirts, dresses.
- Let your children select the clothes they wear for daytime, for sleeping.
- Encourage your children to dress themselves and their

dolls or their stuffed animals.

Have special places for storage.

- Help children put toys away by shape or color, or by use for drawing, for building, for cuddling, for pushing.

Encourage your children to think, imagine, and be creative.

- Ask questions that have many answers, rather than questions that have right or wrong answers, such as "Where do you think birds sleep? How do you think a rainbow gets in the sky? Where do you think the water goes after it goes down the drain?"
- Ask your children to act out a story you've read to them.

Sort and match clothes.

- Ask your children to sort and stack their laundry by putting all like things together such as underwear in one pile, socks in another.
- Let them sort clothes by "owner" (my shirts, Dad's shirts).
- Ask your children to match a shoe with a shoe, a sock with a sock.
- Give your children a limited choice of what to wear. Ask them why they chose the clothes they did.

**In one of the Bathrooms**

The bathroom is a great place for children to learn hygiene and practice using their muscles by brushing their teeth and combing their hair. While they're taking a bath, they can learn math and science concepts, such as sinking and floating, full and empty. Safety tip: Always stay with your children when they're in the bathroom! Put red duct tape on all hot water faucets for safety.

Use mirrors to name body parts.

- Make faces in the mirror with your children—move your tongue, make a kiss, wiggle your nose.
- Talk with your children about all of the things they can do with their eyes—blink, stare, wink.

Look for ways to use different senses in the bathroom.

- Feel and talk about different textures-- soft cotton, hard soap, smooth wall, slippery sink.
- Smell different things—toothpaste, soap.

Let your children play with different things while taking a bath.

- Help your children collect and save things to play with in the bathtub, such as plastic containers, sponges, cartons, and corks.

- ☒ Help your children notice which things sink and float.

Practice helping skills with your children.

- ☒ Encourage your children to wash their hands and face, brush their teeth, and comb their hair.
- ☒ Talk about health and hygiene such as why we wash our hands and face, brush our teeth.

Practice health and safety habits in the bathroom with your children.

- ☒ Let your children practice pouring, washing, wiping up.
- ☒ Talk about do's and dont's such as turning on the cold water first. Tell them what they can touch in the bathroom.
- ☒ Let your children make "warm" water: turning on the cold water first and adding very little hot to prevent burns.

Talk with your children about how it feels to "grow."

- ☒ Hang a growth chart on a door and keep track of their height and weight. Show them how they are growing.
- ☒ Ask them what they can do now that they couldn't do when they were younger and smaller.

Talk with your children about opposites in the bathtub.

- Encourage them to pour water into and out of containers, making them full, making them empty.
- Discover things that are hard and soft, warm and cold, wet and dry.

**In the "Everything/Junk" Drawer**

Every family probably has an "everything/junk" drawer—the one drawer where all the odds and ends are put. When the "everything/junk" drawer is for children, it should be in a safe and accessible location, such as a bottom drawer. This drawer can be a treasure chest! It can be a special treat for a rainy day. Make sure all the items are safe before you give them to your children.

Explore the "everything/junk" drawer.

- Ask your children to put all the like things together, such as corks or rubber bands.
- Ask your children about the uses of the items in the drawers.
- Your children can draw around some of the items to make pictures with the shapes.

Play guessing games with things from the "everything/junk" drawer.

- Hide things in your hands ("What do you think I'm holding in my right hand?").

- Let your children guess amounts ("Will all these corks fit in the cup, or will we need the large bowl?").

Talk about the contents.

- Help your children name all the items in the "everything/junk" drawer.
- Talk about the sizes, shapes, and colors of the items.
- Ask your children about the "feel" of the items—rough or smooth, slippery or sticky, hard or soft.

Create a surprise. Is there anything your children can make from any items in the drawer?

- What about making a collage picture or sculpture with some of the leftover items?
- Let your children surprise you with their own creations.
- Make a mobile by hanging some items from a coat hanger. Place the mobile outside on a tree limb.

Remember clean-up time!

- Using margarine tubs or other small containers, ask your children to clean out, sort, and put back the contents of the drawer.

If your children are preschoolers, let them add to the collections from any "junk" you don't want anymore.

- Corks
- Coffee scoops
- Plastic bottle caps
- Twine
- Ribbon
- Pads of paper
- Buttons
- Greeting cards
- Straws
- Markers
- Tapes
- Rubber bands

**Outside of your Home**

The outdoors! Young children should go outdoors every day for exercise (with weather permitting), fresh air, and fun. You and your children will have greater freedom outdoors to jump, hop, swing, look, and listen. Let your children make noise! Remind them about any rules you have for playing outside.

Talk about all the things you and your young children see in the sky, near the house or apartment

- Colors
- Bright sun
- Moon
- Neighbors

- Cars
- Shapes
- Dark clouds
- Stars
- Snow
- Houses

Help your young children find animals and insects.

- Tell your children the names of the animals and insects they see and hear.
- Ask your children where they think the animals live, how the insects build their homes, where they get their food.

Help your children dig and plant a garden.

- Talk about each tool you are using and what it does.
- Look at seed packages and vegetables in the grocery store. Then, decide what to plant: radishes, carrots, and other things that grow fast and that you and your child like are best.
- Remind your children to water the growing plants.

Look up toward the sky at different times of the day with your young children.

- Talk about the ways that trees bend and what the clouds look like.

- Look for changes over time—how are the leaves different in the fall from the spring? Are there more or less birds in the sky now than there were last month?

Listen for sounds outside.

- Ask your children to talk about the sounds they hear and where they might be coming from.
- Ask them to name sounds that are the same as inside sounds, different from inside sounds.

Encourage your children to describe all the things they feel or experience.

- Rough trees
- Blowing wind
- Slippery mud
- Smooth stones
- Warm air
- Cold rain

**Exploring Your Community**

There are many fun places to go in your community. Before you take a trip, talk with your children about what you will see and do. Name the things and people you will look for, such as flowers, animals, fire fighters, or bus riders in the place you are visiting. Talk with your children about your safety rules so that the trip will be pleasant and safe, such as "I want you to hold my hand."

To a park

- Point out special things in the park: a family having a picnic, the gardens, the pathways.
- While walking around the park, ask your children to walk fast, walk slow, or run safely.
- Play games with your children (that have no "losers").

To the library

- Get your own library card to borrow books.
- Ask your children to select three or four books, records or tapes to check out and take home.
- Remind your children about being quiet at the library.

To the fire station

- Call ahead about coming for a visit.
- Talk about fire safety rules for your home and what your children would do if there was a fire.
- Try on different pieces of the fire fighter's uniform. Ask your children what they think each article of clothing is for, what they think the equipment does.

To the train and/or bus station

- Talk about where the bus or train might be going.
- Make up a story about where you would go on the bus or train. What would you do when you got there?
- Ask your children to tell you what they would do while on the bus or train.

To the grocery store

- Discuss each food item as you put it in the cart: its size, shape, color, and texture.
- Ask your children to name their favorite foods and then name one of yours.
- To keep your children occupied in line, ask questions that have no right or wrong answers, such as: Let's pretend we are having a supper party and you get to choose the menu. "What would you like to serve?"

To a fair, festival and other community event

- Check the listings online for local events or listen to the radio for announcements.
- Talk about the event before you go.
- Try a special new snack as a treat.
- Ask your children to name the two best parts of the event.

On a scavenger hunt

- Decide with your children what you'll look for on the

hunt.
- Use special bags for collections.
- Talk about what is safe to touch and what is not.
- Make up/share a story about the items you collected.

**Things You Can Do After a Trip**

- Talk with your children about what you saw, heard, touched, or smelled.
- Make a booklet about the trip with your children. Have them tell you a story about the trip as you write it down.
- If you take pictures during the trip, put them in a booklet you make or in a photo album.
- Ask your children to add pictures to a "trip book." Let them cut pictures from magazines of things they saw on their trip.
- Make a collage with your children. Use things found during your walk—moss, stones, leaves.
- Get books from the library about where you went.

## Things to Think About

Were the activities you selected fun for you and your family? As you do the activities, they will encourage and help children to learn. They should be fun and offer opportunities for your family to spend meaningful time together. As you remember these activities and plan with your children, it might help you to think about the following:

- Did your children enjoy the activity?
- Which activity did your children enjoy the most? The least?
- Which child enjoyed which activity? Why do you think that's so?
- Which activity seemed too hard? How could you make it easier so that your children can succeed?
- Which activity seemed to be too easy? How could you make it harder so that your children have a challenge?
- Which activity was "just right?" When can you do it again?
- How can you stretch your children's imaginations when you do this or a similar activity?
- What did you learn about your children?
- Ask your children to respond to "What...If" questions related to the activity, such as "What would you have to eat if you lived on the moon?" Or, "What would you do if you worked in this place?"
- What activity can you plan to give your child time to play quietly by himself or herself? Will it help to develop

his or her creativity?
- How did you praise your children for trying a new activity and for their positive behaviors? What other ways can you use to encourage them?
- What other ideas do you have? What ideas can your children suggest?

# Family Fun with older children (Tweens & Teens)

When you are the parent in a houseful of big kids, it will take more than a promise to go to the park a fast food meal to entertain them. Don't get me wrong – I do not feel that it is the parent's job to entertain tweens and teens on their free days off of school, but sometimes it's just as fun for parents to take the time to do something special with their big kids as it is for them.

When your kids were young, they were probably content watching a movie, reading books, or playing games together. But fast forward a few years, and there's a good chance they would rather spend time with friends. Busy schedules can also make it more difficult to find family time as your kids grow up. So, it's important to be proactive about making time to be together.

Whether you're able to schedule fun night once a week or once a month, regular family time can be an important ritual in your growing kid's life. The key is to make family fun night a priority and get everyone in the family involved. If your older child groan when you bring up spending quality time together, make it clear that everyone is going to participate. For one night, don't answer the phone, ignore social media, and step away from your electronics. Make your time together about talking, laughing, and creating new memories. Family activities will give you all an opportunity to get to know one another better so you can maintain a healthy relationship as everyone grows older.

Below are some fun activities that you can do with your tweens and teens that will help create memories that both parent and kid will have for a lifetime.

1. Go to a jump park. Obviously, this depends on the health of everyone involved and the availability of the space, but it's high on our SociallyWize fun activity list since it involves constant physical activity, laughter and no opportunity for your teen to hold their cell phone and ignore you.

2. Go roller skating. Reclaim the fun from your youth by staying upright and balanced while dancing on skates to some of your favorite tunes with your older children.

3. Head to an indoor rock-climbing center if one is in your area.

4. Go bowling. This is a great way to have healthy competition, wage family-friendly bets and use math skills while having fun.

5. Take a class together as a family. Painting with a Twist, an Art class, a cooking class at the local grocery store, a pottery/ceramic class, a self-defense class – what interests do you and your teen share that would be fun to explore together?

6. Start a family book club. Find a book that your children

and you will enjoy and create your own family book club.

7. Go to the dollar movie theater.

8. Go out for ice cream.

9. Make homemade ice cream or popsicles.

10. Go camping as a family.

11. Go swimming as a family.

12. Take a hike in a nearby nature preserve area, that is safe.

13. Do a service project as a family. Volunteer at a local food bank, charity/thrift store/etc.

14. Go to an amusement park as a family. (Six Flags, putt-putt golf, etc.)

15. Start a weekly family fitness routine. Go biking, jogging, walking, playing catch football or something active together on a constant basis.

16. Start a journal together. When my children were younger, we used to have a shared journal. I would write them a question or give them a prompt in a simple spiral notebook. Sometimes it's easier for tweens and teens to say something in a journal than in person.

17. Go to the mall together. This could be fun even if you don't have much money for shopping. Try on silly hats and take photos on your phone or take and text photos of what you'd buy someone if you had the money. It'll make them smile knowing that you're thinking of them.

18. Go antique or thrift store shopping together.

19. Have a family movie marathon evening. This is especially fun if you have a favorite movie series. Make popcorn and/or order pizza and watch a series of movies all in order.

20. Go out for breakfast or make homemade breakfast together.

21. Play a game of family laser tag.

22. Play Frisbee, ultimate frisbee or a solid game of tag in the backyard or front yard space.

23. Head to the Go Kart track together as a family.

24. Go to a paintball event center.

25. Have a family video game marathon. Even though you probably will not know what you are doing, playing video games with your older children will allow them to be the expert and the opportunity to teach their parents a few things.

26. Go to a major or minor league baseball game.

27. Play fun games in the backyard, like basketball, volleyball, or bean bag toss.

28. Have a water gun or balloon competition. (You're never too old for a water gun war.)

29. Ride bikes as a family.

30. Host a big sleepover for their closest friends complete with food and their favorite drinks. Okay, maybe this isn't something you really want to do with them, but it might just get you cool parent points.

# You're a Socially Wize Parent!

Now that you have completed reading this book, I earnestly hope that you have been able to understand my passion for bridging families as well as recognizing ways to bring more mindful balance into your parenting style, as well as advice for connecting with kids at each stage, from infancy to adolescence. My insights and advice comes straight from my heart. I am a work in progress, a learning, evolving parents just like you. I hope that you found some practical, solution-oriented advice in this guide for any parent who longs to end the yelling, power struggles, and downward spiral of acting out, punishment, resentment, and shame--and instead foster an emotional connection that helps kids learn self-discipline, feel confident, and create lasting, loving bonds.

Let's take our last assessment.

1. *What did you learn after completing this book?*
2. *What thoughts or feelings come up for you as you think about the information you have gathered?*
3. *What did you learn about parenting? Or, what is the meaning of this information that is most important to you (and in your work)*
4. *Did you learn anything that can help you parent more effectively?*

I hope that the pages in this book are both consoling and challenging. I hope it reminds you to be a parent who is present, and forgiving, and kind, but most of all you must first be all these things to yourself.

For more information and dialogue, please feel free to visit my website at SociallyWize.com. I am available for individual classes, family sessions and parenting workshops.

# About the Author
Tracey Pugh, M.Ed, Founder Socially Wize Co.

Tracey has over 20 years of experience working in Higher Learning. She is both an energetic and engaging Education leader with proven experience in all aspects of classroom instruction, curriculum development, and parent and student relationships. She excels at developing critical relationships between home and school, as well as high-performing student production to consistently deliver exceptional results.

Tracey brings both a proven track record and perspective to her coaching and classes that include but not limited to the expressive needs surrounding high achieving students and also around those students identified with "high" functioning and non-verbal learning disabilities, ADD/ADHD, and other related social cognitive areas.

As a wife, parent of two thriving college students an educator in private school setting Pugh's career has sustained the tests of life liberty and the pursuit of happiness. She has now made it her mission to make the road to success easier for families of high achieving students.

Tracey has been a confidant to hundreds of families throughout the years. She is also a regionally recognized educator and speaker with a master's degree in education. Her area of expertise is adolescent social, emotional and relational development.

Additional Books by the Author:

Adventures of Lil' Tracey -
Show and Tell